# Wild Thyme
## AND OTHER
## Temptations

# Wild *Thyme* AND OTHER Temptations

THE JUNIOR LEAGUE
OF TUCSON

*Junior League of Tucson, Inc.*
2099 East River Road
Tucson, Arizona 85718
Office 520-299-5753
Fax 520-299-5774
jltucson@aol.com

Library of Congress Number:
00-090075

ISBN: 0-9616403-1-6

*Designed, Edited, and
Manufactured by*
Favorite Recipes® Press
an imprint of

**FRP**™

P. O. Box 305142
Nashville, Tennessee 37230
1-800-358-0560

Book Design: Starletta Polster
Art Director: Steve Newman
Project Manager: Susan Larson

Manufactured in the
United States of America
First Printing: 2000
11,000 copies

## MISSION STATEMENT

*The Junior League of Tucson, Inc. is an organization of
women committed to promoting voluntarism, developing the
potential of women and improving the community through
the effective action and leadership of trained volunteers. Its
purpose is exclusively educational and charitable.*

## 1998–1999 COOKBOOK PRODUCTION COMMITTEE

*Chair*
Karen Palmour

*Sustaining Advisors*
Linda Vala
Grace Murphy

*Fund Development Director*
Kimberly Flack

*Committee Members*
Carolyn Andersen
Stephanie Blonsky
Jennifer Brumley
Mary Catherine Clements
Stacie Cohen
Lisa Groeger
Amy Jo Horner
Deirdre O'Brien-Montijo
Jennifer Riden
Betsey Shepard
Shamra Tankersley
Katie Thompson
Laura Symms Wallace
Susan Weeks

## 1999–2000 COOKBOOK MARKETING COMMITTEE

*Co-Chairs*
Laura Symms Wallace
Kristin Wellik

*Fund Development Director*
Rebecca Sundt

*Sustaining Advisor*
Linda Vala

*Committee Members*
Carolyn Andersen
Carrie Anderson
Diane Ceizyk
Toni Lowery
Kelly McLaughlin
Sacha Reilly
Tiffany Rumel
Kimberly Sundt

# Introduction

*Food comforts us, gives us energy, inspires us. Memories are created around food, with certain aromas evoking specific gatherings—eggs and bacon for the weekend morning family gathering, or onions and garlic sautéing in olive oil as the evening meal begins its preparation, or the bouquet of chocolate cake for a special birthday.... These pleasures are shared with friends and family and all those we hold dear. No wonder we strive to make the food as special as the occasion.*

*Wild Thyme and Other Temptations features over 250 recipes designed to delight the senses. From quick meals to gourmet entrées, from light fare to sinful temptations, this collection of recipes submitted and tested by members of the Junior League of Tucson are sure to meet all your entertaining needs.*

*This book is also designed to give you a "taste" of the Old Pueblo, the original or early Tucson. Tidbits on local history, as well as color photographs of some of our most treasured places, explain why so many of us are proud to call Tucson home. The rich history of the Southwest and its spectacular scenery have inspired artists and chefs alike.*

*Enjoy the tastes and traditions of the Old Pueblo!*

*Proceeds from the sale of this book benefit the charitable endeavors of the Junior League of Tucson, Inc.*

# Table of Contents

# Beginning Temptations

## HORS D'OEUVRE

# Sunset Cocktail Soiree

*Tucson has been voted as one of the best places in the world for sunsets. Our clear vistas and dramatic mountains are the perfect backdrop for the vibrant pinks, oranges, and purples that color the sky. Like the skyline view, the following menu presents a beautiful palette on your plate.*

## Menu

Turkish Red Pepper Spread

Shallot Puffs

Olive Crostini

Chile Relleno Spring Rolls

Spicy Lemon Shrimp

Simple Foie Gras

Champagne and Martinis

# QUICK FRESH TOMATO PIZZAS

### Pizza Crusts

1   envelope fast-rising
    yeast
1   cup warm (100- to
    105-degree) water
1/4  cup olive oil
1/4  cup cornmeal
1   teaspoon salt
3   cups (or more) flour
Cornmeal

### Pizza Topping

2   tablespoons olive oil
2   cups shredded
    mozzarella cheese
1   cup shredded Monterey
    Jack cheese
1/2  cup grated Parmesan
    cheese
4 to 6 Roma or other plum
    tomatoes, sliced
    1/4 inch thick
4   ounces prosciutto or
    Black Forest ham,
    cut into 1/8-inch strips
    (optional)
Salt and freshly ground
    pepper
3 or 4 fresh basil sprigs,
    julienned

*For the crusts,* dissolve the yeast in the water in a large bowl. Add the olive oil, 1/4 cup cornmeal, salt and 3 cups flour, stirring to form a dough. Knead on a floured surface for 5 minutes or until smooth, adding additional flour 1/4 cup at a time if needed to prevent sticking. Place in a greased bowl, turning to coat the surface.

Let rise, covered with plastic wrap, in a warm place for 30 minutes or until nearly doubled in bulk. Divide the dough into 4 portions and shape into disks. Cover with plastic wrap and let rest for 5 to 10 minutes. Stretch and pat the disks into 8-inch circles, forming slightly thicker rims.

Heat baking sheets in a 500-degree oven. Remove the heated baking sheets and sprinkle with additional cornmeal. Arrange the pizza dough rounds on the prepared sheets. Bake at 500 degrees for 5 minutes.

*To top the pizzas,* remove the crusts from the oven and brush with the olive oil. Layer with the cheeses, tomatoes and prosciutto; sprinkle with salt and pepper. Bake for 7 minutes or until the crusts are golden brown and the cheeses are bubbly. Sprinkle with the basil and serve hot with a young red wine.

*Serves sixteen as an appetizer or four as a main course*

# CHILE RELLENO SPRING ROLLS

2 pounds lean ground
   beef, poultry or pork
2 sweet onions, chopped
1 bunch green onions,
   chopped
2 garlic cloves, minced
1 teaspoon ground cumin
Salt and pepper to taste
2 pounds chopped roasted
   green chiles
2 large potatoes, chopped
1 teaspoon chopped
   fresh oregano
4 cups shredded Cheddar
   or Monterey Jack cheese
2 (16-ounce) packages
   won ton wrappers
Vegetable oil for deep-frying

Brown the ground beef in a large saucepan, stirring until crumbly; drain. Add the onions, green onions, garlic, cumin, salt and pepper. Cook until the onions are golden brown, stirring frequently. Add the chiles. Cook for 2 minutes. Add the potatoes and oregano. Cook until the potatoes are tender. Remove from the heat and add the cheese, stirring until the cheese melts. Cool to room temperature.

Place 2 tablespoons of the ground beef mixture in the center of each won ton wrapper. Fold the lower corner of each wrapper over the filling, tucking the end under the filling. Fold over the side corners and roll the wrappers to enclose the filling completely; brush the corners with water and press to seal. Deep-fry the rolls in 325-degree oil in a skillet until golden brown; drain. Serve with hoisin sauce or salsa.

*Makes one-hundred spring rolls*

## Cooking Tips

### HANDLING CHILES

As a general rule, the smaller the chile, the hotter it is. Always wear rubber gloves or rub hands with oil, as the capsaicin can irritate the skin. The irritation can be neutralized by washing hands in a mixture of 1 quart water and 1 tablespoon bleach.

To protect the eyes, do not cut chiles under water. Keep at a safe distance when processing chiles in a food processor, as the blades can disperse the oils and take your breath away.

To lessen the heat of chiles, soak them in ice water for one hour before using. To neutralize the heat on the tongue, place sugar on the tongue or take a drink of any dairy product.

# Mushrooms Stuffed with Sun-Dried Tomatoes

5 dry-pack sun-dried
   tomatoes
18 mushrooms
2 tablespoons olive oil
1/4 cup finely chopped
   shallots
1/3 cup fine dry bread
   crumbs
1 large egg yolk, lightly
   beaten
1/4 cup minced
   fresh parsley
1/2 teaspoon dried basil,
   crumbled
Salt to taste
2 tablespoons grated
   Parmesan cheese

Soak the sun-dried tomatoes in hot water to cover in a small bowl for 5 minutes; drain, reserving 1 tablespoon of the liquid. Remove the stems from the mushrooms and chop fine; reserve the caps.

Heat the olive oil in a small skillet over medium heat until hot but not smoking. Add the chopped mushroom stems and shallots and sauté until the shallots are tender.

Combine the sautéed vegetables, sun-dried tomatoes, bread crumbs, egg yolk, parsley, basil, salt and the reserved soaking liquid in a bowl and mix well. Mound into the reserved mushroom caps.

Arrange in a lightly greased shallow baking pan. Sprinkle with the cheese. Bake at 400 degrees on the center oven rack for 15 minutes.

Serves eighteen

## Other Temptations

### Savory Cheese Wafers

Combine 2 cups shredded sharp cheese, 1 cup flour, 1/2 cup softened butter, 1 teaspoon salt, 1/8 teaspoon cayenne pepper and the desired amount of chopped pecans in a bowl and mix well. Shape into a log about 1 inch in diameter and chill in the refrigerator. Cut into 1/4-inch slices and arrange on a baking sheet lined with baking parchment. Bake at 300 degrees for 20 to 25 minutes or until crisp and golden brown; for a crisp wafer, do not underbake.

# SHALLOT PUFFS

8  ounces shallots,
   finely chopped
1  tablespoon olive oil
1/2  teaspoon crumbled
   dried sweet basil
1/4  teaspoon sugar
1/4  cup finely shredded
   Swiss cheese
1/2  cup cold water
2  tablespoons unsalted
   butter
3/8  teaspoon salt
1/2  cup flour
3  eggs, beaten
1  teaspoon water
1  egg

Sauté the shallots in the heated olive oil in a large skillet over medium-high heat for 3 minutes or until tender-crisp. Add the basil, sugar and cheese, and stir until the cheese melts; set aside.

Combine 1/2 cup water, butter and salt in a heavy large saucepan. Bring to a boil, stirring to melt the butter; remove from the heat. Beat in the flour with a wooden spoon. Return to the heat and cook until the mixture forms a ball, stirring constantly. Cool for 1 minute. Beat in the 3 beaten eggs 1/4 at a time at low speed. Add the shallots and beat until smooth.

Drop by rounded teaspoonfuls 1 1/2 inches apart on buttered baking sheets. Whisk 1 teaspoon water with the remaining egg in a small bowl. Brush lightly over the tops of the puffs. Bake at 425 degrees for 20 minutes or until golden brown.

NOTE: PUFFS MAY BE STORED IN AN AIRTIGHT CONTAINER IN THE REFRIGERATOR FOR UP TO 3 DAYS OR FROZEN FOR UP TO 3 MONTHS. REHEAT AT 350 DEGREES FOR 10 MINUTES TO SERVE.

*Makes four dozen*

# TEX-MEX DEVILED EGGS

6    hard-cooked eggs
1    tablespoon finely
     chopped green onions
1    tablespoon chopped
     cilantro or parsley
1    small serrano or
     jalapeño chile
1/4  cup mayonnaise or
     mayonnaise-type
     salad dressing
1    teaspoon prepared
     mustard
1/4  cup shredded
     Cheddar cheese

Cut a thin slice from each end of the eggs so they will stand upright. Cut the eggs into halves crosswise. Remove the yolks to a small bowl and mash well. Add the green onions, cilantro, chile, mayonnaise and mustard and mix well.

Spoon the yolk mixture into the egg whites. Top with cheese and garnish with chili powder. Store, covered, in the refrigerator until serving time.

*Serves twelve*

# CHICKEN TIKKA

2 to 3 tablespoons plain
     yogurt
1    tablespoon lemon juice
1    ounce tikka seasoning
1/2  teaspoon paprika
1/2  teaspoon garlic powder
1/2  teaspoon ground ginger
1/2  teaspoon salt
2    pounds boneless
     skinless chicken breasts
2    tablespoons butter,
     melted

Combine the yogurt, lemon juice, tikka seasoning, paprika, garlic powder, ginger and salt in a bowl and mix well. Cut the chicken into 1-inch cubes; add to the yogurt mixture, stirring to coat well. Marinate in the refrigerator for 8 hours or longer; drain.

Place the chicken in 2-quart baking dish. Bake or broil for 10 to 12 minutes or until cooked through, turning once and basting with the melted butter.

NOTE: TIKKA SEASONING CAN BE FOUND IN INDIAN MARKETS OR THE SPICE SECTION OF LARGE SUPERMARKETS. NUTRITIONAL ANALYSIS DOES NOT INCLUDE TIKKA SEASONING.

*Serves twelve*

# SALSA VERDE CHICKEN PASTRY

4 or 5 cooked chicken
    breasts, chopped
1    (16-ounce) can black
    beans, drained,
    coarsely mashed
1/3  cup salsa verde
2    (12-inch) pie pastries,
    at room temperature
1    cup shredded
    Cheddar cheese
1/4  cup sliced green onions
1    egg
1    tablespoon water

Combine the chicken, beans and salsa verde in a medium bowl and mix well. Place 1 pastry on a greased 12-inch round baking pan. Spoon the chicken mixture over the pastry, leaving a 1-inch edge. Sprinkle with the cheese and green onions.

Beat the egg and water in a small bowl; brush over the edge of the pastry. Top with the remaining pastry and seal the edge with the tines of a fork. Prick the top pastry and brush with the remaining egg wash. Bake at 400 degrees for 40 minutes or until golden brown. Let stand for 10 minutes. Cut into 16 wedges and serve topped with sour cream and a sprig of cilantro if desired.

*Serves sixteen*

## Beverage Tips

### GOLF MARTINIS

Combine 8 parts gin with 2 parts dry vermouth in a shaker. Add angostura bitters to taste and cracked ice and shake well. Strain into chilled cocktail glasses and add a cocktail olive to each glass.

# MUSSELS IN CREAM SAUCE

60 mussels, about
    4 pounds
1  cup dry white wine
2  tablespoons minced
   shallots
1  tablespoon minced
   parsley
1  tablespoon minced
   celery leaves
2  tablespoons butter
2/3 cup light cream or
   half-and-half
1  tablespoon butter

Scrub the mussels well, discarding any that are open or broken. Combine with the wine, shallots, parsley, celery leaves and 2 tablespoons butter in a large saucepan. Cover and bring to a boil over high heat. Remove the cover and remove the mussels with a slotted spoon as soon as they open, reserving the cooking liquid. Keep the mussels warm, discarding the empty top shells.

Boil the cooking liquid until it is reduced by half. Boil the cream in a small saucepan until thickened and syrupy. Stir the cream into the mussel cooking liquid. Stir in 1 tablespoon butter and remove from the heat. Add the mussels. Serve from a chafing dish or in serving bowls with thick slices of French bread. Garnish with additional parsley.

NOTE: SCRUBBED MUSSELS CAN BE HELD IN COLD WATER IN THE REFRIGERATOR FOR UP TO 24 HOURS.

Serves eight

## Other Temptations

### REUBEN RYE TOASTS

Drain one 15-ounce can sauerkraut and press to remove the excess moisture. Combine with 2 cups shredded Swiss cheese, 1 cup shredded Cheddar cheese and 10 ounces shredded corned beef in a bowl. Add 1/4 cup mayonnaise, or enough to bind the mixture. Spoon into an 8 × 8-inch baking dish and bake at 350 degrees for 20 minutes. Serve on rye toasts.

# SEARED SEA SCALLOPS IN VODKA AND LEEK SAUCE

3　tablespoons butter
12　large sea scallops
White portions of 2 leeks,
　chopped
1/4　cup vodka
1/2　teaspoon salt
1/2　teaspoon pepper

Heat 1 tablespoon of the butter in a skillet over medium-high heat until sizzling. Add the scallops and cook for 1 minute or until the outsides are seared, but the centers are not cooked through. Remove with a slotted spoon and set aside.

Reduce the heat and add the leeks to the skillet. Sauté for 3 to 4 minutes or until tender. Add the vodka and scallops. Cook for 1 to 2 minutes or until the vodka has been reduced. Add the remaining butter 1 tablespoon at a time, cooking until the sauce has thickened and the scallops are cooked through, stirring constantly. Season with salt and pepper.

*Serves four*

# BASS ALE SHRIMP

2　(12-ounce) cans
　dark beer
1　bay leaf
1 1/2　tablespoons
　mustard seeds
1/2　teaspoon dillseeds
1/4 to 1/2 teaspoon dried red
　pepper flakes
1/4　teaspoon salt
4　whole peppercorns
1 1/2　pounds medium
　unpeeled shrimp
1/4　cup vinegar
2　garlic cloves, crushed

Combine the beer, bay leaf, mustard seeds, dillseeds, pepper flakes, salt and peppercorns in a saucepan. Bring to a boil and reduce the heat. Simmer for 5 minutes. Add the shrimp. Cook for 2 to 4 minutes or until the shrimp turn pink.

Pour into a glass bowl. Add the vinegar and garlic. Chill in the refrigerator for 2 hours or longer. Drain the shrimp, discarding the bay leaf. Mound in the center of a lettuce-lined serving plate. Garnish with a circle of black olives.

*Serves eight*

# SPICY LEMON SHRIMP

4   *quarts water*
1   *large lemon, sliced*
5   *pounds unpeeled*
    *large shrimp*
2   *cups vegetable oil*
1   *tablespoon olive oil*
1/4  *cup hot sauce*
1   *tablespoon minced*
    *garlic*
1<sup>1</sup>/2 *teaspoons minced*
    *fresh parsley*
1<sup>1</sup>/2 *teaspoons dried*
    *oregano leaves*
1<sup>1</sup>/2 *teaspoons dried*
    *thyme leaves*
1<sup>1</sup>/2 *teaspoons dried*
    *basil leaves*
1<sup>1</sup>/2 *teaspoons seafood*
    *seasoning*
1<sup>1</sup>/2 *teaspoons salt*

Bring the water and lemon slices to a boil in a large saucepan. Add the shrimp and cook for 3 to 5 minutes or until the shrimp turn pink; drain and let stand until cool. Peel the shrimp.

Combine the vegetable oil, olive oil, hot sauce, garlic, parsley, oregano, thyme, basil, seafood seasoning and salt in a large nonreactive bowl and whisk until smooth. Add the shrimp, tossing to coat well.

Marinate the shrimp, covered, in the refrigerator for 8 hours. Drain and serve in a lettuce-lined bowl.

*Serves twenty-five*

# ARTICHOKE-STUFFED BAGUETTE

1    baguette sweet bread
1/2   cup (1 stick) butter
2    tablespoons
     sesame seeds
3 or 4 garlic cloves, chopped
1 1/2 cups sour cream
2    cups shredded
     Monterey Jack cheese
1/4   cup grated Parmesan
     cheese
1    (15-ounce) can
     artichoke hearts,
     drained, cut into
     quarters
2    tablespoons
     parsley flakes
2    teaspoons lemon pepper
1    cup shredded
     Cheddar cheese

Cut a slice off the top of the bread and scoop out the center to form a shell; cut the center bread into cubes and reserve.

Melt the butter in a skillet and add the reserved bread cubes, sesame seeds and garlic. Cook until the bread cubes and sesame seeds are toasted, tossing to toast evenly. Add the sour cream, Monterey Jack cheese, Parmesan cheese, artichokes, parsley flakes and lemon pepper and mix well.

Spoon the mixture into the bread shell. Place on a baking sheet. Bake at 350 degrees for 25 minutes. Sprinkle with the Cheddar cheese and bake for 5 minutes longer. Let stand until cool and slice to serve.

*Serves twelve*

---

## Beverage Tips

### ABOUT CHAMPAGNE

A magnum of Champagne, which is the equivalent of two bottles, may be a better choice for entertaining, because Champagne ages more gently in a larger bottle. To open Champagne, hold the bottle at a 45-degree angle and twist the bottle while holding the cork. This will control the cork from popping and prevent the Champagne from overflowing.

# CURRANT AND CRANBERRY BRIE

1/3  cup chopped dried
     cranberries
1/3  cup chopped dried
     currants or raisins
1/3  cup chopped walnuts
2    tablespoons apple jelly
1    (8-ounce) round of
     Brie cheese
2    sheets frozen puff
     pastry, thawed
1    egg white
2    tablespoons water

Combine the cranberries, currants, walnuts and apple jelly in a bowl and mix well.

Cut off the top of the Brie and scoop out enough of the center to hold the cranberry mixture; reserve the top. Spoon the cranberry mixture into the cheese shell and replace the top.

Roll 1 sheet of the puff pastry large enough to wrap the cheese. Place the cheese in the center and fold the pastry to enclose the cheese completely. Cut desired shapes from the remaining sheet of pastry and decorate the top. Place on a baking sheet.

Beat the egg white with the water in a small bowl. Brush over the pastry. Bake at 375 degrees for 25 minutes or until golden brown.

*Serves ten*

# OLIVE CROSTINI

20   thin slices French bread
10   pitted kalamata olives
10   pitted green olives
1/4  cup chopped fresh basil
2    garlic cloves
1/4  cup olive oil

Place the bread slices on a baking sheet. Toast in a 350-degree oven until crisp. Purée the olives with the basil, garlic and olive oil in a blender or food processor. Spread about 1 teaspoon of the olive mixture on each toast.

*Serves twenty*

# SAN XAVIER DEL BAC

Mission San Xavier del Bac is located just south of Tucson and is affectionately referred to as
the White Dove of the Desert. It is the oldest continuously active mission in the United States and is
still a spiritual center for the Tohono O'odham Reservation, with services held daily.
Father Eusebio Francisco Kino, a Jesuit missionary who came to the area in 1692, laid out the foundation
of the first church in 1700. That church was destroyed, and the mission we see today was started
by the Franciscans in 1783 and completed by 1797. San Xavier incorporates Spanish, Byzantine, and
Moorish architecture, and is one of the finest examples of mission construction in the country.

# Roasted Tomato and Eggplant Crostini

1  large red onion
2  tablespoons balsamic or
   red wine vinegar
1¹/₂ pounds Roma tomatoes
1  medium eggplant
Salt and pepper to taste
16  (¹/₂-inch) slices French
    or Italian bread

Spray two 10 × 15-inch baking pans with olive oil cooking spray. Cut the onion into ¹/₂-inch slices. Arrange the slices in a single layer in 1 of the baking pans. Drizzle with the vinegar. Cut the tomatoes into ¹/₄-inch slices. Arrange in the pan with the onion slices, overlapping slightly. Cut the unpeeled eggplant crosswise into ¹/₂-inch slices. Arrange the slices in the second baking pan. Spray all the vegetables with additional cooking spray.

Roast the eggplant at 450 degrees for 30 minutes or until tender golden brown. Roast the onions and tomatoes for 50 minutes or until the tomatoes are browned on the edges. Combine the vegetables in a blender or food processor container and process until smooth. Season with salt and pepper.

Arrange the bread slices on a baking sheet. Broil 5 inches from the heat source until toasted on both sides. Spoon the vegetable mixture onto the toasts.

NOTE: FOR A LESS FAT-CONSCIOUS APPETIZER, BRUSH THE BREAD WITH OLIVE OIL OR BUTTER BEFORE TOASTING AND TOP THE VEGETABLE MIXTURE WITH FETA OR GOAT CHEESE. THE VEGETABLE MIXTURE MAY BE PREPARED IN ADVANCE AND STORED IN THE REFRIGERATOR FOR UP TO 3 DAYS.

Serves sixteen

# SMOKED BLACK BEAN AND CORN SPREAD

8 to 10 slices bacon
1   medium onion, chopped
4 or 5 garlic cloves, chopped
2   (15-ounce) cans
     black beans
$^1/2$  cup water
2   tablespoons vinegar
$^1/2$  teaspoon pepper
2   cups cooked whole-
     kernel corn
15  ounces Monterey Jack
     cheese, shredded

Fry the bacon in a skillet until crisp. Remove the bacon to drain and pour off all but 2 to 4 tablespoons of the drippings; crumble the bacon and reserve. Add the onion to the skillet and sauté until golden brown. Add the garlic and sauté until tender. Add the bacon and 1 can of the beans. Rinse the bean can with $^1/4$ cup of the water and add to the skillet.

Purée the remaining beans with the remaining $^1/4$ cup water in a blender or food processor. Add to the skillet with the vinegar and pepper. Bring to a boil and reduce the heat. Simmer for 15 minutes or until thickened.

Spread the mixture on a heatproof serving platter. Spread the corn over the top and sprinkle with the cheese. Heat in the oven or microwave just until the cheese melts. Serve with tortilla chips.

*Serves sixteen*

## Other Temptations

### CHEESY RYE TOASTS

Toast 2 loaves of party rye bread lightly on both sides and spread with butter. Mix $2^1/2$ cups shredded Cheddar cheese, $1^1/2$ cups sliced black olives, $^3/4$ cup sliced green onions and $^3/4$ cup mayonnaise in a bowl. Spread on the toasted bread and place on baking sheets. Broil for 2 to 3 minutes or until bubbly and serve warm.

# SIMPLE FOIE GRAS

1   envelope unflavored
    gelatin
1/4  cup cold water
1   (10-ounce) can beef
    consommé
8   ounces braunschweiger
8   ounces cream cheese,
    softened
3   green onions, chopped
1/2 to 1 teaspoon
    Worcestershire sauce
1/4  teaspoon dry mustard

Soften the gelatin in the cold water. Bring the consommé to a boil in a saucepan. Add the gelatin and stir until completely dissolved. Pour 1/3 of the mixture into a shallow 9-inch dish or mold. Chill until firm.

Combine the braunschweiger and cream cheese in a bowl and mix until smooth, using your hands if necessary. Add the green onions, Worcestershire sauce and dry mustard; mix well. Stir in the remaining gelatin mixture. Pour over the congealed layer.

Chill for 4 hours or longer, until completely firm. Place the bottom of the dish in hot water just long enough to loosen and invert onto a serving plate. Serve with crackers or toast rounds.

*Serves twelve*

# ROASTED PEPPER AND ARTICHOKE TAPENADE

1   (7-ounce) jar roasted
    red bell peppers
1   (6-ounce) jar
    marinated artichoke
    hearts
1/2   cup minced fresh
    parsley
1/3   cup olive oil
1/4   cup drained capers
4   garlic cloves, chopped
1   tablespoon lemon juice
1/2   cup grated Parmesan
    cheese
Salt and pepper to taste

Drain the bell peppers and artichoke hearts and chop coarsely. Combine with the parsley, olive oil, capers, garlic, lemon juice and cheese in a food processor container and process until finely chopped.

Combine with salt and pepper to taste in a bowl and mix well. Serve immediately on crackers or crostini or store in the refrigerator for up to 24 hours.

*Serves twelve*

## Cooking Tips

### ARTICHOKES

Dip into fiber! More people should be on familiar terms with this unusual vegetable. It contains an amazing amount of fiber, with 5.2 grams for a medium artichoke. That's more than a whole bowl of oat-bran cereal. And with only 53 calories in a medium artichoke, it's a good choice for the health-conscious diner.

# PESTO CHEESECAKE

1    tablespoon butter,
      softened
1/4   cup fine dry bread
      crumbs
2    tablespoons grated
      Parmesan cheese
16   ounces cream cheese,
      softened
1    cup ricotta cheese
1/2   cup grated Parmesan
      cheese
1/4   teaspoon salt
1/8   teaspoon cayenne
      pepper
3    large eggs
1/2   cup pesto
1/4   cup pine nuts
1/4   cup finely chopped
      sun-dried tomatoes

Spread the butter over the bottom and side of a 9-inch springform pan. Sprinkle with a mixture of the bread crumbs and 2 tablespoons Parmesan cheese.

Combine the cream cheese, ricotta cheese, 1/2 cup Parmesan cheese, salt and cayenne pepper in a large mixing bowl and beat until light. Beat in the eggs 1 at a time. Spoon about half the mixture into a medium bowl. Stir the pesto into the remaining cheese mixture.

Spoon the pesto mixture into the prepared springform pan and smooth the top. Spoon the remaining cheese mixture carefully over the pesto layer and smooth the top. Sprinkle with the pine nuts and sun-dried tomatoes.

Bake at 325 degrees for 45 minutes or until the center appears set when the pan is shaken. Cool completely on a wire rack. Chill, tightly covered with plastic wrap, for 8 hours or longer. Loosen the side of the cheesecake from the pan with a sharp knife. Place on a serving plate and remove the side of the pan. Garnish with fresh basil and serve with crackers.

*Serves sixteen*

## Beverage Tips

### HOLIDAY CHEER BEVERAGE

For a hit at your next holiday open house or winter party, combine 2 quarts hot apple cider with 1/4 cup maple syrup and 1/4 cup sugar in a punch bowl and stir to dissolve the sugar. Add 1 cup lemon juice and 1 quart golden rum. Float apples studded with cloves in the punch and garnish with cinnamon sticks.

# BUTTERY SALMON SPREAD

7 ounces smoked salmon
4 teaspoons lemon juice
1/2 teaspoon Dijon mustard
1/4 teaspoon hot
   pepper sauce
1/4 cup (1/2 stick) butter,
   melted, cooled
1/2 cup sour cream

Combine the salmon, lemon juice, Dijon mustard and pepper sauce in a blender or food processor container. Process until puréed. Add the butter and sour cream and process until smooth. Serve with bagel chips or toast rounds.

*Serves eight*

# TURKISH RED PEPPER SPREAD

1/4 cup chopped walnuts
1 (7-ounce) jar roasted
   red bell peppers,
   drained
1/2 cup fresh bread crumbs
1 large garlic clove,
   crushed
1 1/2 teaspoons ground
   cumin
1/4 teaspoon red
   pepper flakes
Salt to taste
1 tablespoon extra-virgin
   olive oil
1 tablespoon (or more)
   fresh lemon juice

Toast the walnuts in a small skillet until fragrant, shaking to prevent burning; cool. Combine with the bell peppers, bread crumbs, garlic, cumin, pepper flakes and salt in a food processor container and process until finely chopped.

Add the olive oil and lemon juice and process until smooth. Adjust the lemon juice and seasonings to taste. Serve with toasted pita wedges or sesame crackers.

*Serves twelve*

# Spinach Madeline

2   (10-ounce) packages
    frozen chopped spinach,
    thawed
1/4  cup (1/2 stick) butter
2   tablespoons flour
2   tablespoons
    chopped onion
1   garlic clove, minced
1/2  cup light cream
2   cups shredded jalapeño
    cheese
1   teaspoon
    Worcestershire sauce
3/4  teaspoon celery seeds
Red pepper and black pepper
    to taste
Corn bread stuffing mix or
    cracker crumbs

Drain the spinach well, reserving 1/2 cup liquid. Melt the butter in a heavy saucepan over low heat. Stir in the flour. Cook for 2 to 3 minutes or until bubbly but not brown, stirring constantly. Add the onion and garlic and cook until tender but not brown. Stir in the reserved spinach liquid and cream. Add the cheese, Worcestershire sauce, celery seeds, red pepper and black pepper. Cook until the mixture thickens and the cheese melts, stirring constantly. Add the spinach and mix well.

Spoon into a buttered baking dish. Top with the stuffing mix. Bake at 350 degrees for 15 to 20 minutes or until bubbly. Serve with corn chips or crackers.

NOTE: THIS CAN ALSO BE SERVED AS A VEGETABLE OR SIDE DISH.

Serves sixteen as an appetizer or six as a side dish

# GARLIC HUMMUS

1¹/2 cups dried chick-peas
3   medium garlic cloves
Juice of 2 medium lemons
³/4  cup tahini
Dash of tamari
¹/4  cup packed minced
     fresh parsley
¹/4  cup minced scallions
1¹/2 teaspoons salt
Cayenne pepper and black
     pepper to taste

Soak the chick-peas in water to cover in a bowl for 1¹/2 hours; drain. Combine with fresh water to cover in a saucepan and cook for 1¹/2 hours or until very tender; drain. Process the chick-peas to a thick paste in a food processor or food mill.

Combine with the garlic, lemon juice, tahini, tamari, parsley and scallions in a bowl. Season with salt, cayenne pepper and a generous amount of black pepper and mix well. Chill until serving time. Adjust the seasonings. Garnish with green or black olives, chopped tomatoes and chopped cucumbers. Serve with crackers or pita bread.

NOTE: TAHINI IS A SESAME BUTTER WITH THE CONSISTENCY OF PEANUT BUTTER. TAMARI IS A DARK SAUCE MADE FROM SOYBEANS; IT IS SIMILAR TO BUT THICKER THAN SOY SAUCE.

Serves six

## Other Temptations

### MUSHROOM DIP

Chop 1 pound mushrooms fine and place in a skillet heated to 250 degrees. Cook for 1 hour or longer. Add ¹/2 cup chopped onion and 1 chicken or beef bouillon cube. Cook until all the liquid has evaporated. Stir in 1¹/2 cups sour cream and cook on low heat for 20 minutes. Add 8 ounces cream cheese and cook until the cream cheese melts, stirring to mix well. Add the juice of 1 lemon and enough flour to thicken to the desired consistency. Cook until smooth and thick, stirring constantly. Serve from a chafing dish with crackers.

# WARM CRAB AND ARTICHOKE DIP

1/4   cup cream cheese,
      softened
1/2   cup mayonnaise
Salt and pepper to taste
3/4   cup drained cooked
      crab meat, about
      4 ounces
1/4   cup grated Parmesan
      cheese
3     tablespoons drained
      chopped marinated
      artichoke hearts
2     tablespoons sliced
      green onions
2     tablespoons chopped
      red bell pepper
2     tablespoons
      chopped celery
1     tablespoon finely
      chopped Italian parsley
1 1/2 teaspoons sherry
      wine vinegar
1/2   teaspoon hot
      pepper sauce
2     tablespoons grated
      Parmesan cheese

Beat the cream cheese in a large mixing bowl until smooth. Add the mayonnaise and beat just until blended. Season with salt and pepper. Fold in the crab meat, 1/4 cup Parmesan cheese, artichoke hearts, green onions, bell pepper, celery, parsley, vinegar and hot pepper sauce with a spatula.

Spoon the mixture into a 2-cup soufflé dish. Top with 2 tablespoons Parmesan cheese. Bake at 400 degrees for 15 minutes or until the crab mixture is heated through and the cheese melts. Serve immediately with toasted baguette slices.

*Serves ten to fifteen*

# SHRIMP DIP

1   pound unpeeled
    medium shrimp
Salt to taste
8   ounces cream cheese,
    softened
1/3   cup finely chopped red
    bell pepper
1/3   cup finely chopped
    onion
3   tablespoons chopped
    fresh parsley
3   tablespoons chopped
    fresh dill
1/2   teaspoon horseradish
3 1/2   tablespoons fresh
    lemon juice
1/4   cup mayonnaise
1/4   cup sour cream
1/4   teaspoon salt
1/8   teaspoon cayenne
    pepper

Cook the shrimp in salted boiling water in a saucepan for 3 minutes or just until pink; drain and cool. Peel, devein and chop the shrimp. Combine with the cream cheese, bell pepper, onion, parsley, dill and horseradish in a bowl.

Add the lemon juice, mayonnaise, sour cream, 1/4 teaspoon salt and cayenne pepper and mix well. Chill, covered, for several hours. Serve with crackers, vegetables or toast.

*Serves sixteen*

## Other Temptations

### JENKINS POINT CRAB DIP

Combine 1 pound cooked fresh lump crab meat, 4 cups shredded mild Cheddar cheese, 1/2 cup grated onion, 3/4 cup minced celery, the juice of 1 lemon, 5 dashes Tabasco sauce and salt and pepper to taste in a bowl. Add enough Hellman's mayonnaise to bind and mix well. Chill until serving time and serve with crackers.

# Temptations du Jour

SOUPS & ACCOMPANIMENTS

## CHARITY LUNCHEON

*Helping hands and hearts are in abundance when it comes to Tucson charities and causes, including efforts of the Junior League of Tucson. Ronald McDonald House, Parent Connection, and Big Brothers/Big Sisters are just a few of the organizations the League has supported in its more than 65-year history. What better way to kick off a fund-raiser than with a generous luncheon?*

## *Menu*

### LOBSTER BISQUE

### THYME CHICKEN IN PASTRY

### SUN-DRIED TOMATO AND MUSHROOM FETTUCCINI

### APPLE NUT MUFFINS

### CHOCOLATE CHEESECAKE

### ICED TEA AND COFFEE

# SOPA DE ALBONDIGAS

1 egg
1 tablespoon milk
1 pound lean ground beef
1/2 cup uncooked rice
1/2 slice dry bread, crumbled
4 garlic cloves, finely chopped
1 teaspoon oregano
1 teaspoon chopped fresh mint (optional)
1 teaspoon salt
1 teaspoon pepper
1 medium onion, finely chopped
1 medium tomato, seeded, chopped

Beat the egg with the milk in a small bowl. Combine with the ground beef, rice, bread crumbs, garlic, oregano, mint, salt and pepper in a large bowl. Add half the onion and tomato. Shape into 1-inch meatballs.

Bring water to a rolling boil in a large saucepan. Add the meatballs 1 at a time, keeping the water at a boil. Add the remaining onion and tomato. Simmer for 30 minutes after the last meatball is added. Adjust the seasonings. Serve with chopped cilantro and salsa.

NOTE: IF THE WATER IS NOT MAINTAINED AT A BOIL AS THE MEATBALLS ARE ADDED, THEY TEND TO FALL APART.

Serves six

## Tucson Times

### TUCSON BOTANICAL GARDENS

The Tucson Botanical Gardens offer 5½ acres for viewing and learning about plants indigenous to the area. The herb garden peaks from April through June; the wildflower garden blooms from March through May; cactus plants are at their prime from April through August; and the native American crops are best from May through August.

# HUNGARIAN GOULASH SOUP

1   *pound beef shoulder*
*or shank*
2   *tablespoons paprika*
1   *teaspoon cayenne*
*pepper*
1   *teaspoon caraway seeds*
2   *medium onions,*
*chopped*
6   *tablespoons*
*vegetable oil*
2   *garlic cloves*
1   *green bell pepper, cut*
*into strips*
4   *Roma tomatoes,*
*chopped*
1   *tablespoon tomato paste*
1/2   *teaspoon marjoram*
6   *cups (about) beef stock*
2   *medium potatoes,*
*peeled, chopped*
*Salt and pepper to taste*

Cut the beef into 1/2-inch cubes. Mix the paprika, cayenne pepper and caraway seeds in a bowl. Add the beef cubes and toss to coat well. Sauté the onions in the heated oil in a large heavy saucepan until translucent. Add the beef and sauté until light brown.

Add the garlic, bell pepper, tomatoes, tomato paste, marjoram and enough stock to cover the beef. Simmer for 1 hour, adding additional stock as needed to cover the beef. Add the potatoes, salt and pepper. Simmer for 25 minutes longer or until the potatoes are tender.

Skim the soup and discard the garlic. Adjust the seasonings and serve with a dollop of sour cream.

*Serves eight*

# Eggplant Minestrone

1    medium onion, chopped
2    tablespoons olive oil
1    pound ground sirloin
1    medium eggplant,
      chopped
2    garlic cloves, minced
1/2  cup chopped carrot
1/2  cup chopped celery
2    (14-ounce) cans peeled
      Roma tomatoes
2    (14-ounce) cans
      beef broth
1    teaspoon sugar
1/2  teaspoon nutmeg
1    teaspoon salt
1/2  teaspoon pepper
2    tablespoons minced
      parsley
1/2  cup grated Parmesan
      cheese

Sauté the onion in the heated olive oil in a skillet for 3 minutes. Add the ground sirloin and cook until brown and crumbly, stirring constantly; drain.

Combine the beef mixture with the eggplant, garlic, carrot, celery, tomatoes, beef broth, sugar, nutmeg, salt and pepper in a large stockpot. Cook over medium heat for 30 minutes or until the vegetables are tender. Sprinkle servings with the parsley and Parmesan cheese and serve with bagel chips.

*Serves eight*

# LENTIL AND SAUSAGE SOUP

1¹/2 cups dried lentils
1 medium onion, chopped
6 cups water
1¹/2 teaspoons chopped
    fresh rosemary, or
    ¹/2 teaspoon dried
    rosemary
1 pound mushrooms,
    sliced
2 tablespoons olive oil
12 ounces sweet and/or
    hot Italian sausage
¹/2 cup water
¹/2 cup chopped fresh
    parsley
1¹/2 teaspoons salt
¹/2 teaspoon pepper

Rinse and sort the lentils. Combine with the onion and 6 cups water in a large saucepan and bring to a boil. Add the rosemary and reduce the heat. Simmer for 30 minutes.

Sauté the mushrooms in the heated olive oil in a skillet for 5 minutes or until golden brown. Remove to a dish with a slotted spoon. Pierce the skin of the sausage and add to the skillet with ¹/2 cup water. Cook over medium-high heat until the water evaporates and the sausage is brown, turning frequently. Drain and cool the sausage; cut into slices.

Add the mushrooms, sausage, parsley, salt and pepper to the lentils in the saucepan. Simmer for 10 minutes longer.

*Serves four*

## Beverage Tips

### HOMEMADE SANGRIA

To liven up your next party, mix 4 cups of a chilled, light red wine with ³/4 cup brandy or vodka and ¹/2 cup superfine sugar in a pitcher and stir to dissolve the sugar. Add 2 cups sparkling water, the slices of 1 orange and 1 lemon, and 6 to 8 strawberries just before serving. Add a splash of orange juice to each glass if desired.

# SPICY TOMATO AND SAUSAGE SOUP

1¹/2 pounds medium-spicy
    Italian sausage
2    garlic cloves, minced
2    onions, chopped
1    pound tomatoes,
    peeled, cored, or
    1 (16-ounce) can
    Italian plum tomatoes
1¹/2 cups dry red wine
6    cups beef broth
¹/2  teaspoon dried basil
¹/2  teaspoon dried oregano
3    tablespoons chopped
    fresh parsley
1    medium green bell
    pepper, chopped
    (optional)
2    medium zucchini, sliced
    ¹/4 inch thick
1    cup uncooked
    spinach pasta
Salt and pepper to taste
¹/2  cup grated Parmesan
    cheese

Remove the casings from the sausage and break into bite-size pieces. Cook in a heavy stockpot until light brown. Remove the sausage to paper towels to drain; pour all but 3 tablespoons drippings from the stockpot.

Add the garlic and onions to the stockpot and sauté for 2 to 3 minutes or until tender. Add the tomatoes, stirring to break up. Add the wine, beef broth, basil and oregano. Simmer for 30 minutes. Skim the soup. Add the parsley, bell pepper, zucchini, pasta, salt, pepper and sausage. Simmer, covered, for 25 minutes longer. Serve with the Parmesan cheese.

*Serves ten*

## About Thyme

### QUALITY THYME
There are believed to be about 100 different species of thyme. It is one of the great culinary herbs of European cuisine. Its flavor blends well with other herbs, especially rosemary. Thyme is an herb that aids the digestion of fatty foods and is particularly good in lamb, goose, and duck dishes.

# CURRIED CHICKEN AND THYME SOUP

4    *boneless skinless*
      *chicken breasts*
2    *ribs celery, cut into*
      *4-inch pieces*
4    *large carrots, sliced*
      *diagonally*
1/2   *medium yellow onion,*
      *coarsely chopped*
2 to 3 *teaspoons (or more)*
      *curry powder*
1/2   *teaspoon thyme*
1/2   *teaspoon basil*
1    *teaspoon ground or*
      *crumbled sage*
2    *teaspoons salt*
1/2   *teaspoon pepper*
6    *cups water*
3    *chicken bouillon cubes*
4    *cups uncooked*
      *instant rice*

Combine the chicken with the celery, carrots, onion, curry powder, thyme, basil, sage, salt and pepper in a large saucepan. Add the water and chicken bouillon cubes and cook for 30 minutes or until the chicken is tender. Remove the chicken from the saucepan, reserving the cooking liquid. Cool the chicken slightly and cut or shred into bite-size pieces. Return to the saucepan. Discard the celery ribs or cut into bite-size pieces and return to the saucepan.

Adjust the seasonings and add the rice. Simmer for 10 minutes. Serve with crackers.

NOTE: YOU MAY SUBSTITUTE 3 CANS OF CHICKEN BROTH AND ENOUGH WATER TO MEASURE 6 CUPS FOR THE WATER AND BOUILLON CUBES. TO VARY THE SOUP, USE BROWN RICE AND/OR ADD 1/2 TEASPOON ROSEMARY AND 1/2 TEASPOON GARLIC.

*Serves six*

# LOBSTER BISQUE

1/4  cup (1/2 stick) butter
1/4  cup flour
1  teaspoon tomato paste
1/2  teaspoon paprika
Freshly ground nutmeg
     to taste
4  cups half-and-half
1  cup chopped cooked
   lobster meat
1/2  cup cream sherry
Salt and white pepper
     to taste

Melt the butter in a heavy saucepan over medium heat. Sprinkle the flour into the butter and stir to blend well. Reduce the heat and cook for 5 minutes, stirring constantly; do not brown. Stir in the tomato paste, paprika and nutmeg.

Whisk in the half-and-half. Bring to a boil and cook until thickened, stirring constantly. Add the lobster meat and sherry. Reduce the heat and simmer for 5 minutes. Season with salt and white pepper and serve immediately.

*Serves six*

# SOPA CALABACITAS

8  zucchini, chopped
5  tomatoes, seeded,
   chopped
2  bunches green onions,
   chopped
1  garlic clove, crushed
2  cups fresh, canned or
   frozen corn kernels
4  cups water
10  chicken bouillon cubes
1  pound longhorn cheese,
   shredded

Steam the zucchini, tomatoes and green onions in a saucepan for 10 minutes or until tender. Combine with the garlic, corn, water and bouillon cubes in a stockpot. Cook for 15 minutes. Add the cheese and simmer for 10 minutes longer, stirring to melt the cheese completely.

NOTE: YOU MAY SUBSTITUTE 4 CUPS CHICKEN BROTH FOR THE WATER AND BOUILLON CUBES.

*Serves six to eight*

# BARRIO HISTORICO

This historic neighborhood is also known as Barrio Libre, or Free Neighborhood. It earned the name "free" in the early 1800s, when Anglo law was not enforced in the area.

The neighborhood features more than 150 old adobe homes, making it one of the best collections of such structures in the world.

One of the most interesting features of the neighborhood is El Tiradito, or The Wishing Shrine. The story goes that a gambler who became enamored with the wife of another man was mortally shot by the enraged husband. The gambler staggered away to die on the spot that is now El Tiradito.

Neighbors lit candles for the gambler's soul, and eventually candles were lit and prayers said for others. The belief emerged that if the candle stayed lit all night the prayer would be answered. In 1940 a wall was constructed to protect the shrine, which is the only shrine known to exist in North America that is dedicated to a sinner.

# Sonoran Black Bean Soup with Jalapeño Chiles

1    pound dried
     black beans
1/4  cup olive oil
1    onion, chopped
2    carrots, chopped
3    garlic cloves, chopped
1/2  jalapeño chile
1    tablespoon cumin
     seeds, toasted, ground
1 1/2 teaspoons ground
     cardamom
2    bay leaves
1    cup dry white wine
1 1/2 teaspoons chili powder
4    cups chicken broth
Dash of wine vinegar
Salt and freshly ground
     pepper to taste

Rinse and sort the beans. Combine with water to cover in a bowl and let stand for 8 hours. Drain and rinse.

Heat the olive oil in a stockpot over medium heat. Add the onion, carrots, garlic and jalapeño chile. Reduce the heat and cook, covered, for 7 to 10 minutes or until the vegetables are tender but not brown. Add the cumin, cardamom and bay leaves. Cook over medium heat for 2 minutes. Stir in the wine and chili powder. Cook until the liquid is reduced by half.

Add the beans and chicken broth. Bring to a boil and reduce the heat; skim off the foam. Simmer for 1 hour or until the beans are very tender; discard the bay leaves. Season with vinegar, salt and pepper. Garnish servings with sour cream and chopped tomato.

NOTE: FOR A QUICKER SOUP, BRING THE BEANS TO A BOIL AND COOK FOR 5 MINUTES. REMOVE FROM THE HEAT AND LET STAND FOR 1 HOUR. FOR A THICKER SOUP, PURÉE HALF THE COOKED BEANS AND VEGETABLES.

Serves six to eight

# CALDO DE QUESO

1   large onion, chopped
4   large potatoes, peeled,
    chopped
2   medium tomatoes,
    peeled, chopped
6 to 8 chiles, roasted,
    peeled, chopped
2   tablespoons butter
1   tablespoon vegetable oil
1   (14-ounce) can
    chicken broth
4   cups water
Salt and pepper to taste
12  ounces Monterey Jack
    cheese, cut into
    1/2-inch cubes
1 or 2 tablespoons
    evaporated milk, or
    to taste

Sauté the onion, potatoes, tomatoes and chiles in the butter and oil in a large saucepan until the onion is tender. Add the chicken broth, water, salt and pepper. Simmer, covered, until the potatoes are tender.

Add the cheese, stirring to melt evenly. Stir in the evaporated milk.

NOTE: YOU MAY SUBSTITUTE 1 MEDIUM AND 1 SMALL CAN WHOLE GREEN CHILES FOR THE FRESH PEPPERS.

Serves six

## Cooking Tips

### CANNED GREEN CHILES

Hot peppers fire up dishes from the American Southwest, and several kinds can be found canned. They are generally milder than the fresh chiles. The best known are jalapeños—fat, oval chiles with blunt, tapered ends. They are meaty chiles with smooth dark green skins that redden as they ripen. Milder Anaheim chiles from California and bolder new Mexican chiles are also canned. Both are fleshier and larger than jalapeños, with sweet, earthy flavors and a cutting heat. Any of these can be used in recipes calling for canned green chiles.

# SPICY TROPICAL GAZPACHO

1/2 cup chopped peeled
mango
1/2 cup chopped peeled
papaya
1/2 cup chopped peeled
fresh pineapple
1/2 cup chopped,
seeded peeled
cucumber
1/4 cup chopped green
bell pepper
1/4 cup chopped red
bell pepper
2 tablespoons minced
fresh cilantro
1 cup tomato juice
1 cup pineapple juice
1/2 to 1 teaspoon hot
pepper sauce
1/4 teaspoon salt

Combine the mango, papaya, pineapple, cucumber, bell peppers and cilantro in a food processor or blender container. Add the tomato juice, pineapple juice, hot pepper sauce and salt. Pulse 4 times or just until coarsely chopped. Chill, covered, until serving time.

*Serves four*

# CREAM OF POBLANO PEPPER SOUP

12 ounces poblano chiles
3/4 cup chopped onion
3/4 cup chopped celery
1/4 cup (1/2 stick) butter
1/2 cup flour
4 cups chicken stock
4 cups cream or
    half-and-half
Salt and pepper to taste

Grill the chiles. Let stand until cooled. Peel, seed and chop the chiles; wear rubber gloves to protect your skin.

Sauté the onion and celery in the butter in a stockpot until tender. Add the flour. Cook until light brown, stirring constantly; do not overbrown.

Heat the chicken stock in a large saucepan. Whisk into the flour mixture. Cook until thickened, stirring constantly. Add the grilled chiles and simmer for 30 minutes. Cool slightly. Purée the mixture in a blender. Return to the stockpot.

Heat the cream in a medium saucepan. Add enough to the puréed mixture to make the desired consistency. Season with salt and pepper. Garnish servings with chopped cilantro.

*Serves six to eight*

## Cooking Tips

### GRILLED PEPPERS

To grill peppers, rub all sides with oil and place on an oiled grill rack. Grill over hot coals until the skin is blistered and charred on all sides, turning frequently; do not burn. Place in a sealable plastic bag and seal. Let stand until cool. Peel, seed and chop the peppers when cool. Wear rubber gloves for hot peppers to protect the skin.

# HEARTY POTATO AND CORN CHOWDER

3    carrots, sliced
1    large potato, chopped
1    green onion,
     thinly sliced
1    (10-ounce) package
     frozen French-style
     green beans
1    (10-ounce) package
     frozen lima beans
2    cups water
1    (16-ounce) can cream-
     style corn
1    (16-ounce) can whole
     kernel corn
1/4  teaspoon celery seeds
1/8  teaspoon thyme
1    teaspoon salt
1/8  teaspoon pepper
2    cups half-and-half
     or milk
1    cup shredded sharp
     Cheddar cheese
3    tablespoons butter

Combine the carrots, potato, green onion, green beans and lima beans with the water in a saucepan. Cook for 10 minutes or until the vegetables are tender-crisp.

Add the cream-style corn, whole kernel corn, celery seeds, thyme, salt and pepper. Stir in the half-and-half, cheese and butter. Simmer for 20 minutes or until the vegetables are tender, stirring occasionally; do not allow to boil.

*Serves ten*

# SOPA DE TORTILLA

12  corn tortillas
Vegetable oil for frying
Salt to taste
1  medium tomato,
    peeled, seeded, chopped
1  small onion, chopped
1  garlic clove, crushed
1  tablespoons chopped
    fresh cilantro, or
    1/2 teaspoon ground
    coriander
1  (7-ounce) can green
    chile salsa
1  tablespoon vegetable oil
6  cups chicken broth
1  cup shredded
    longhorn cheese
1  cup shredded Monterey
    Jack cheese

Cut the tortillas into strips. Fry in oil in a skillet until crisp; drain and sprinkle with salt.

Combine the tomato, onion, garlic, cilantro and salsa in a blender container and process until finely chopped. Sauté the mixture in 1 tablespoon heated oil in a saucepan until slightly reduced. Add the chicken broth and bring to a boil.

Sprinkle the tortilla strips into soup bowls and top with a mixture of the cheeses. Spoon the soup into the bowls. Serve with avocado, chopped cooked chicken, cilantro sprigs or chiles if desired.

Serves four to six

## Cooking Tips

### ABOUT CHEESE

Many cheeses come stamped with a "sell by" date on the package. In general, the softer the cheese, the shorter the storage life. If there is no date on the container, soft cheeses should be stored no longer than five days after purchase. Firm and hard cheeses have less moisture and can be stored for several weeks.

# MC's Barbecue Sauce

1    pound (4 sticks) butter
     or margarine
1    (10-ounce) bottle
     Worcestershire sauce
2    tablespoons
     Tabasco sauce
1    cup prepared mustard
2    cups vinegar
Juice and grated zest of
     3 lemons
Salt, cayenne pepper and
     black pepper to taste

Melt the butter in a saucepan. Add the Worcestershire sauce, Tabasco sauce, mustard, vinegar, lemon juice, lemon zest, salt, cayenne pepper and black pepper and mix well.

Place on the grill to keep warm to baste chicken, pork, ribs, steaks or any grilled meat. Store unused portions in the refrigerator.

*Makes six cups*

# Classic Béarnaise Sauce

$1/2$   cup white wine
1    tablespoon finely
     chopped shallots
$1^{1}/2$ teaspoons tarragon
2    egg yolks
1    tablespoon heavy cream
$3/8$   teaspoon salt
$1/2$   cup (1 stick) unsalted
     butter

Combine the wine, shallots and tarragon in a small saucepan. Cook until the wine is reduced to a glaze consistency. Combine the egg yolks, heavy cream and salt in a blender container. Add the wine mixture gradually, pulsing until well blended.

Melt the butter in a small saucepan and heat until bubbly. Add to the wine mixture in a steady stream, processing until the sauce thickens.

NOTE: YOU MAY SERVE IMMEDIATELY, OR KEEP WARM IN A DOUBLE BOILER OVER WARM WATER UNTIL SERVING TIME.

*Makes one and one-half cups*

# SOUTHWEST CRANBERRY SAUCE

Minced zest of 1 orange
3/4   cup water
1/2   cup sugar
2     tablespoons minced
      gingerroot
1     (12-ounce) package
      fresh cranberries
Juice of 1 orange
Juice of 2 limes
2     tablespoons sugar
1/2   bunch cilantro,
      finely chopped
3     serrano chiles, minced
1 1/2 tablespoons rum

Combine the orange zest, water, 1/2 cup sugar and gingerroot in a small saucepan. Cook over medium-high heat until thick and syrupy, stirring frequently.

Chop the cranberries in a food processor. Combine with the syrup mixture in a small bowl. Add the orange juice, lime juice, 2 tablespoons sugar, cilantro, chiles and rum and mix well. Chill for 24 hours for the best flavor.

Serves twelve

---

## Tucson Times

### HOHOKAM

Prehistoric Indians that archeologists call the Hohokam occupied parts of Arizona from 300 B.C. to 1450 A.D. Remnants of their sophisticated agricultural community are found throughout the Tucson area. Pot shards, irrigation canals, tools, and adobe dwellings are just a few of the reminders that ours was not the first culture to discover this region.

# LEMON HERB SAUCE

1/4 cup olive oil
5 ounces plain yogurt
5 ounces sour cream
1/2 teaspoon fresh
  lemon juice
1 tablespoon Dijon
  mustard
1 tablespoon chopped
  fresh tarragon
1 teaspoon chopped fresh
  parsley
Salt and pepper to taste

Combine the olive oil, yogurt, sour cream, lemon juice and Dijon mustard in a blender container. Add the tarragon and parsley. Pulse until well mixed. Season with salt and pepper. Serve over asparagus.

*Serves four to six*

# MUSTARD DILL SAUCE

1/2 cup sugar
1 cup chopped fresh dill,
  or 1 1/2 teaspoons
  dried dill
1 cup Dijon mustard
1/3 cup wine vinegar
1/2 cup mayonnaise
2 tablespoons
  vegetable oil

Mix the sugar and dill in a small bowl. Add the Dijon mustard, vinegar and mayonnaise and mix well. Stir in the oil gradually. Serve over cold poached salmon.

*Serves sixteen*

# MESQUITE BEAN JELLY

3   quarts mesquite beans
4$^1$/2 cups sugar
$^1$/4   cup lemon juice
1    package powdered
      pectin
Red food coloring (optional)
Paraffin

Break each mesquite bean into 2 or 3 pieces and combine with water to cover in a large saucepan. Simmer until the water turns yellow. Strain the mixture and reserve 3 cups liquid.

Combine the reserved liquid with the sugar, lemon juice and pectin in a large saucepan. Bring to a rolling boil over high heat, stirring constantly. Boil for 1 minute. Remove from the heat and skim off the foam with a metal spoon. Add the food coloring if desired. Pour quickly into sterilized jars.

Melt the paraffin in a saucepan and spoon over the hot jelly immediately. Let stand until cool.

*Makes six jelly jars*

## Other Temptations

### SALSA RELISH

Combine 1 seeded and chopped large tomato, $^1$/2 cup chopped onion, $^1$/4 to $^1$/2 cup chopped and seeded pickled jalapeño chiles, 1 can drained and rinsed black beans, 1 can drained Mexicorn or whole kernel corn, 2 minced garlic cloves, $^1$/4 cup chopped cilantro and $^1$/2 teaspoon salt in a bowl and mix well. Chill until serving time to blend flavors. Serve with fish, chicken, or steak or with chips as a dip.

# Mango Tomatillo Salsa

15 tomatillos
1/2 cup pineapple juice
1/4 cup white wine vinegar
5 garlic cloves, chopped
Juice of 2 limes
1/4 cup (or more) chopped
    cilantro
1 teaspoon red
    pepper flakes
3 firm ripe mangoes,
    chopped
1 red onion, chopped
1 red bell pepper, chopped
Chopped jalapeño chiles
    to taste

Combine the tomatillos, pineapple juice, vinegar, garlic, lime juice, cilantro and red pepper flakes in a blender container. Process until puréed.

Combine the puréed mixture with the mangoes, onion, bell pepper and chiles in a bowl. Garnish with additional chopped cilantro.

Serves ten

## Other Temptations

### Black Bean Salsa

Drain and rinse 2 cans black beans. Combine with 2 chopped tomatoes, 4 sliced green onions, 1 chopped garlic clove, 3 tablespoons chopped fresh cilantro, 2 tablespoons fresh lime juice, 1/4 teaspoon salt and 1/4 teaspoon pepper in a bowl. Chill for 8 hours. Drain well and serve with tortilla chips.

# POMEGRANATE SALSA

1   large pomegranate or
    2 medium
    pomegranates
1   large orange
1   green onion, thinly
    sliced
1 to 3 teaspoons minced
    jalapeño chile
1   tablespoon chopped
    fresh cilantro
2   teaspoons fresh
    lime juice
1/4   teaspoon ground cumin
Salt to taste

Break the pomegranate into large pieces and place in water to cover in a bowl. Let stand until seeds can be easily released. Drain, reserving only the seeds; pat the seeds dry.

Cut the peel from the orange. Hold the orange over a bowl and cut between the segments to release the sections. Squeeze the juice from the membranes and discard the membranes. Cut the sections into bite-size pieces.

Add the pomegranate seeds, green onion, chile, cilantro, lime juice and cumin and mix well. Season with salt. Serve immediately or store in the refrigerator.

*Serves four*

# SPINACH PESTO

Leaves of 1 bunch spinach
1 cup fresh parsley leaves
1/4 cup fresh basil
6 garlic cloves
2/3 cup grated Parmesan
cheese
1/2 cup walnuts or
pine nuts
1/2 teaspoon anise or
fennel seeds
1 teaspoon dried tarragon
1 teaspoon salt
1/2 teaspoon freshly ground
pepper
1 cup olive oil

Combine the spinach, parsley leaves, basil, garlic, cheese, walnuts, anise, tarragon, salt and pepper in a blender container. Process until smooth. Add the olive oil in a thin stream, processing until smooth. Adjust the seasonings.

Chill until serving time or store in the refrigerator for up to 1 week. Serve over pasta, pizza, French bread or vegetables.

*Makes two cups*

## Other Temptations

### CILANTRO LIME MAYONNAISE

Combine 1/4 cup mayonnaise, 1 tablespoon finely chopped cilantro, 1 tablespoon lime juice and 1/2 teaspoon finely shredded lime zest in a bowl and mix well. Chill, covered, until serving time.

# SUN-DRIED TOMATO MISO SAUCE

2   garlic cloves, minced
2   tablespoons olive oil
2   tablespoons unsalted
    butter
1   tablespoon finely
    chopped fresh basil
1   teaspoon finely chopped
    fresh rosemary
2   tablespoons chopped
    drained oil-pack
    sun-dried tomatoes
1   tablespoon light
    yellow miso
1/2   cup chicken broth
1/4   cup heavy cream

Sauté the garlic in the olive oil and butter in a skillet until tender. Add the basil, rosemary and sun-dried tomatoes. Bring to a simmer, stirring constantly.

Whisk the miso and chicken broth in a small bowl. Add to the sun-dried tomato mixture. Cook until the mixture is reduced to a syrupy consistency. Reduce the heat to medium-low and whisk in the cream. Return to a simmer. Serve over pasta or roasted chicken.

*Makes one cup*

# Lighter
# Temptations

## SALADS & DRESSINGS

# SUMMERTIME PICNIC

*Mount Lemmon in the Santa Catalina Mountains reaches
9,157 feet high. Pine trees, lakes, campgrounds, and picnic sites
make the mountain summits a favorite place for Tucson
residents to escape the heat of the desert in the summer or to enjoy
skiing in the winter. No matter if the weather is hot or
cold, this menu is the perfect match for casual surroundings.*

## Menu

TEX-MEX DEVILED EGGS

WALNUT AND GORGONZOLA SALAD

SANTA FE STEAK SALAD

WHEAT GERM MUFFINS

CHOCOLATE CRINKLES

RASPBERRY LEMONADE AND BEER

# CILANTRO AND BELL PEPPER
# FARFALLE SALAD

1   cup coarsely chopped
    cilantro
2¹/2 cups chopped green
    bell peppers
2¹/2 cups chopped tomatoes
1   cup finely chopped
    onion
1   (8-ounce) can chopped
    green chiles
4   teaspoons minced garlic
1   cup grated Parmesan
    cheese
1   cup olive oil
3   tablespoons lime juice
2   teaspoons salt
1   teaspoon freshly
    ground pepper
1¹/2 pounds farfalle pasta,
    cooked, drained

Combine the cilantro, bell peppers, tomatoes, onion, chiles, garlic and cheese in a large bowl. Add the olive oil, lime juice, salt and pepper and mix well.

Add the pasta and toss to coat well. Serve immediately or store, covered, in the refrigerator until serving time. Let stand until room temperature and toss again to serve.

*Serves twelve*

# FIESTA PASTA SALAD

### Fiesta Dressing

- 1/2 cup olive oil
- 1/2 cup red wine vinegar
- 2 teaspoons minced garlic
- 1 tablespoon chili powder
- 2 teaspoons ground cumin

### Salad

- 12 ounces uncooked rotelle
- 1 cup chopped red onion
- 1 cup chopped red bell pepper
- 1 (8-ounce) can whole kernel corn, drained
- 1 (4- or 7-ounce) can chopped green chiles
- 1 to 2 tablespoons chopped jalapeño chiles
- 1/4 cup chopped fresh cilantro or parsley

*For the dressing,* whisk the olive oil, vinegar, garlic, chili powder and cumin together in a small bowl.

*For the salad,* cook the pasta using the package directions; drain. Let stand until cooled. Combine the pasta, onion, bell pepper, corn, chiles and cilantro in a large bowl and mix well. Add the dressing and toss to coat well. Chill for 30 minutes or longer before serving.

*Serves six*

## Cooking Tips

### COOKING PASTA

To cook one pound of pasta, bring four quarts water to a full boil. Add 2 tablespoons salt and the pasta. Fresh pasta will be ready when the water returns to a full boil. Dried pasta will take longer, depending on the size and shape. Drain the pasta in a colander, combine with sauce and toss to serve.

# SESAME AND CILANTRO
# VERMICELLI SALAD

**Honey Soy Dressing**

1/4 cup corn oil

3 tablespoons sesame oil

1 teaspoon crushed dried
red pepper, pepper oil
or chili powder

3 tablespoons honey

2 tablespoons soy sauce

1 teaspoon salt

**Salad**

8 ounces thin vermicelli,
thin spaghetti or angel
hair pasta

1 tablespoon salt

2 tablespoons coarsely
chopped cilantro

1/4 cup chopped roasted
peanuts

1/4 cup thinly sliced
green onions

1 tablespoon toasted
sesame seeds

*For the dressing,* combine the corn oil, sesame oil and red pepper in a microwave-safe dish. Microwave on High for 2 minutes. Add the honey, soy sauce and salt and mix well.

*For the salad,* cook the pasta with the salt in boiling water in a large saucepan for 8 minutes or until tender; drain, but do not rinse.

Combine the pasta with the dressing in a bowl and toss to coat well. Chill, covered, for up to 12 hours. Add the cilantro, peanuts and green onions and toss to mix. Sprinkle with the sesame seeds and garnish with additional cilantro leaves.

*Serves ten to twelve*

# SPAGHETTI VINAIGRETTE

**Red Wine Vinaigrette**
- 1/2 cup olive oil
- 1/2 cup red wine vinegar
- 3/4 teaspoon salt
- Freshly ground pepper
    to taste

**Salad**
- 16 ounces spaghetti
- Salt to taste
- 10 Italian plum tomatoes, chopped
- 3/4 cup chopped red onion
- 1 small bunch arugula or spinach, coarsely chopped

*For the vinaigrette,* combine the olive oil, vinegar, salt and pepper in a covered jar and shake to mix well. Store in the refrigerator no longer than 24 hours for maximum flavor.

*For the salad,* cook the spaghetti al dente in salted boiling water in a large saucepan; drain. Combine with the vinaigrette in a large bowl and toss to coat well. Add the tomatoes, onion and arugula and toss to mix. Garnish with green onions.

*Serves six*

## About Thyme

### HERB VINEGARS

To make herb vinegars, pour good-quality white or red wine vinegar over a generous handful of fresh herbs in a jar and let stand, covered, for two weeks. To speed the process, the vinegar can be slightly heated first. Strain out the herbs before using if desired. Try tarragon in cider vinegar; green and red basil in red wine vinegar; and dill flowers, chive blossoms, lemon zest, garlic, oregano, mint, rosemary, or wild thyme in white vinegar.

# CURRIED CHICKEN AND PASTA SALAD

<sup>1</sup>/2  cup chopped onion
2   tablespoons
    vegetable oil
2   teaspoons curry powder
<sup>1</sup>/2  cup mayonnaise
<sup>1</sup>/2  cup plain yogurt
3   tablespoons chutney
<sup>1</sup>/2  teaspoon salt
2   cups chopped cooked
    chicken
1   cup seedless grape
    halves
1   cup chopped cantaloupe
<sup>1</sup>/2  cup chopped celery
5   ounces shell pasta,
    cooked, drained

Sauté the onion in the oil in a skillet until transparent. Add the curry powder and sauté for 2 minutes longer. Combine with the mayonnaise, yogurt, chutney and salt in a bowl and mix well.

Add the chicken, grapes, cantaloupe, celery and pasta and toss to mix well. Chill until serving time.

*Serves eight*

## Other Temptations

### CLASSIC CHICKEN SALAD

To serve ten, cook 5 chicken breasts until tender; cool and chop. Combine with 2 cups chopped celery, 8 ounces chopped pecans and 2 cups red grape halves in a bowl. Whip 2 cups of whipping cream and add to the salad with 1<sup>1</sup>/2 cups or more mayonnaise and mix gently. Season with salt and pepper and garnish the servings with paprika.

# Santa Fe Steak Salad

**Salad**

1¹/₂ teaspoons chili powder
1¹/₂ teaspoons ground
    cumin
1    teaspoon salt
¹/₂ teaspoon freshly ground
    pepper
1    (1- to 1¹/₂-pound)
    boneless sirloin steak,
    1 inch (or more) thick
1    tablespoon vegetable oil
1    medium red onion,
    chopped
1    tablespoon vegetable oil
Fresh corn kernels from
    4 ears, or 10 ounces
    frozen corn
2    medium tomatoes,
    seeded, chopped
2    jalapeño chiles, seeded,
    chopped
3    tablespoons chopped
    fresh basil

**Steak Dressing**

Reserved pan juices
3    tablespoons
    vegetable oil
2    tablespoons red wine
    vinegar
Salt and pepper to taste

*For the salad*, combine the chili powder, cumin, salt and pepper in a small bowl and mix well. Trim the steak and rub with 1 tablespoon oil and the spice mixture. Let stand while preparing the vegetables.

Sauté the onion in 1 tablespoon oil in a skillet for 1 minute. Add the corn. Cook for 3 to 5 minutes. Combine with the tomatoes, chiles and basil in a large bowl and toss gently.

Place the steak in a roasting pan. Roast at 500 degrees for 15 to 18 minutes for medium-rare or until done to taste. Let stand for 10 minutes. Cut into thin strips, reserving the pan juices.

*For the dressing*, combine the reserved pan juices with the oil and vinegar in a bowl. Season with salt and pepper.

*To serve*, arrange the vegetable mixture on serving plates. Top with the steak slices and drizzle with the dressing.

*Serves four*

# SOUTHWESTERN BEEF SALAD

**Steak Marinade**

| | |
|---|---|
| 3 | tablespoons vegetable oil |
| 2 | tablespoons lime juice |
| 2 | tablespoons soy sauce |
| 1 | tablespoon water |
| 1$^1$/4 | teaspoons lemon pepper |
| 1 | teaspoon garlic powder |

**Salad**

| | |
|---|---|
| 1 | pound sirloin steak, cut into strips |
| 6 | cups assorted salad greens |
| 1 | red bell pepper, cut into strips |
| 1 | yellow bell pepper, cut into strips |
| 1 | green onion, sliced |
| | Guacamole |
| | Tortilla chips |

*For the marinade*, combine the oil, lime juice, soy sauce, water, lemon pepper and garlic powder in a sealable plastic bag and mix well.

*For the salad*, add the steak strips to the marinade. Let stand for 15 minutes, turning occasionally. Heat a skillet and add the steak with the marinade. Cook for 2 to 3 minutes or until done to taste, stirring constantly.

Arrange the salad greens on plates. Spoon the steak strips over the greens. Top with the bell pepper strips and green onion. Dollop with guacamole and sprinkle with crushed tortilla chips to serve.

*Serves four*

# ARIZONA-SONORA DESERT MUSEUM

The Arizona-Sonora Desert Museum is enjoyed each year by about 600,000 visitors from all over the world. Its unique feature is that it is a living museum. Insects, reptiles, animals, and birds found in the Sonoran Desert live inside exhibits that are microcosms of their natural habitats. Plant communities, from the desert grasslands to the mountains, are replicated in this one outdoor museum.

The museum opened in 1952 as a way of showing visitors and locals alike the wonders of the desert that surrounds them. William Carr, one of the museum's founders, was hopeful that after gaining an appreciation for the desert, people would be less likely to abuse the landscape and its resources.

One of the favorite animals to observe is the mountain lion, and it is the symbol and mascot for the Desert Museum.

# Avocado and Potato Salad with Horseradish

2 pounds new potatoes
1/4 cup olive oil
1 1/2 tablespoons red wine
   vinegar
Salt to taste
1/2 cup sour cream
1/2 cup plain yogurt
2 tablespoons prepared
   horseradish
1/4 cup loosely packed,
   stemmed fresh
   dill sprigs
3 ribs celery, cut into
   1/4-inch pieces
2 firm medium avocados
1 tablespoon fresh
   lime juice
Freshly ground pepper to taste

Steam the potatoes for 20 minutes or until tender. Cool slightly and cut into 1-inch pieces. Mix the olive oil and vinegar with salt to taste in a large bowl. Add the potatoes and toss to coat well. Cool to room temperature, tossing occasionally.

Whisk the sour cream, yogurt and horseradish together in a small bowl. Stir in the dill. Add to the potatoes with the celery and toss to coat well.

Cut the avocados into 1-inch pieces. Toss with the lime juice in a small bowl. Add the avocados and lime juice to the potatoes and toss lightly to coat well. Season with salt and pepper. Serve immediately or chill for 30 minutes before serving.

*Serves six to eight*

## Cooking Tips

### About Avocados

The most common varieties of avocados are the dark bumpy-skinned Baas and the larger, smoother, thin-skinned Fuerde. Avocados should be used as soon as they are peeled, as they darken quickly when peeled. Chilling avocados will also cause them to darken. Placing the avocado pit in the prepared dish until serving time will help slow discoloration, as will covering the dish with lemon slices, lime slices, or plastic wrap placed directly on the surface. To keep chopped avocados from discoloring, float them in water with lemon juice and drain before using. To speed ripening, place avocados in a paper bag.

# AVOCADO AND MOZZARELLA SALAD

4 plum tomatoes,
   chopped
1/4 cup pitted kalamata
   olives
3 tablespoons julienned
   fresh basil leaves
1/4 cup olive oil
3 to 4 tablespoons rosemary
   or tarragon vinegar
1 tablespoon balsamic
   vinegar
1 avocado, chopped
1 cup coarsely chopped
   drained water-pack
   mozzarella cheese
Salt and freshly ground
   pepper

Combine the tomatoes, olives, basil, olive oil, herb vinegar and balsamic vinegar in a bowl and mix well. Chill, covered, for 2 to 24 hours. Add the avocado and mozzarella cheese and mix gently. Season with salt and freshly ground pepper.

*Serves four*

# BROCCOLI SALAD

1/2 cup golden raisins
Florets of 2 pounds broccoli
1 cup red seedless
   grape halves
3 green onions,
   thinly sliced
2/3 cup mayonnaise
2 tablespoons cider
   vinegar
1/4 cup slivered almonds
8 slices bacon, crisp-
   fried, crumbled

Soak the raisins in hot water to cover in a bowl for 5 minutes; drain. Combine with the broccoli, grapes and green onions in a bowl and mix well.

Mix the mayonnaise and vinegar in a small bowl. Add to the broccoli mixture and mix well. Chill, covered, for several hours. Add the almonds and bacon and toss lightly just before serving.

*Serves six to eight*

# CITRUS BEAN SALAD

$^1/_2$  cup olive oil
$^1/_4$  cup red wine vinegar
1   teaspoon sugar
2   (11-ounce) cans
    mandarin oranges,
    drained
1   (19-ounce) can
    garbanzo beans, drained
1   (19-ounce) can red
    kidney beans, drained
$^1/_2$  cup very thinly sliced
    red onion
$^1/_4$  cup chopped parsley

Whisk the olive oil, vinegar and sugar together in a bowl. Add the mandarin oranges, garbanzo beans, kidney beans, onion and parsley and toss to mix well. Chill until serving time.

*Serves eight*

# CAYENNE SLAW

**Cayenne Dressing**
1   cup mayonnaise
$^1/_2$  cup chopped
    green onions
3   tablespoons apple
    cider vinegar
$^3/_4$  tablespoon chili powder
$^1/_2$  teaspoon ground cumin
$^1/_2$  teaspoon cayenne
    pepper

**Slaw**
1   large head cabbage
3   carrots (optional)
$^1/_2$  cup grated jicama
Salt and pepper to taste
$^3/_4$  cup toasted pecans

*For the dressing,* combine the mayonnaise, green onions, vinegar, chili powder, cumin and cayenne pepper in a bowl and mix well.

*For the slaw,* grate the cabbage and carrots and mix with the jicama in a bowl. Add the dressing and mix well. Season with salt and pepper. Chill until serving time. Sprinkle with the pecans to serve.

*Serves ten*

# FRESH CORN AND CILANTRO SALAD

**Cilantro Dressing**

| | |
|---|---|
| 2/3 | cup chopped fresh cilantro |
| 1/4 | cup red wine vinegar |
| 2 | tablespoons minced shallots |
| 1 | tablespoon minced seeded jalapeño chile |
| 4 | teaspoons olive oil |
| 1/4 | teaspoon salt |
| 1/8 | teaspoon pepper |

**Salad**

| | |
|---|---|
| 5 | cups fresh corn kernels |
| 1 1/2 | cups finely chopped onions |
| 1 1/2 | cups chopped red bell pepper |
| 1 | tablespoon minced gingerroot |
| 4 | garlic cloves, minced |

*For the dressing,* combine the cilantro, vinegar, shallots, chile, olive oil, salt and pepper in a covered jar and shake to mix well.

*For the salad,* combine the corn, onions, bell pepper, gingerroot and garlic in a bowl and mix well. Heat a large nonstick skillet sprayed with olive oil cooking spray until medium-hot. Add the corn mixture and sauté for 8 minutes or until the corn begins to brown.

Combine the corn mixture and the dressing in a bowl and toss to coat well. Chill, covered, until serving time.

*Serves eight*

---

## About Thyme

### ABOUT CILANTRO

Cilantro is the green leaves of the coriander plant and is widely used both cooked and fresh in Latin American, Caribbean, and Asian cooking. Cilantro can be stored in a plastic bag in the refrigerator for up to 1 week. To stretch the time, place the entire bunch with the stems down in a container of water and cover tightly, changing the water every 2 or 3 days. Drain and pat dry before using.

# ENDIVE AND JICAMA TOSS

4 large navel oranges
5 tablespoons toasted
   pine nuts
1/4 cup peanut oil
2 tablespoons rice vinegar
Salt and pepper to taste
4 large heads Belgian
   endive, each cut into
   8 wedges
2 1/2 cups julienned jicama
4 Anaheim chiles,
   seeded, sliced
6 tablespoons crumbled
   Gorgonzola cheese
1/4 cup packed chopped
   fresh cilantro
3 tablespoons toasted
   pine nuts

Grate 1 1/2 tablespoons orange zest from 1 of the oranges and reserve. Cut the peel from the oranges. Hold the oranges over a bowl and cut between the membranes to release the sections, reserving the sections and 3 tablespoons orange juice.

Combine the reserved orange juice and grated orange zest with 5 tablespoons pine nuts, peanut oil and vinegar in a blender container and process until smooth for the dressing. Season with salt and pepper.

Combine the orange sections with the endive, jicama, chiles, cheese and cilantro in a large bowl. Drizzle with the dressing and toss to coat well. Sprinkle with 3 tablespoons pine nuts.

*Serves four to six*

---

## Cooking Tips

### BEYOND ICEBERG

Experiment with a variety of lettuces. Try Batavia, a compact head with soft tender leaves; mix it with Boston, romaine, endive. watercress, or radicchio. Bibb and Boston are soft heads with loose leaves that lend themselves well to lining salad bowls or platters. Endive, or chicory, has crisp, curly green leaves and a pale heart; it can be bitter when old. Frisée has frilly light green leaves with firm white ribs and a slightly bitter taste; mix it with arugula, oak leaf lettuce, and radicchio. Radicchio has deep crimson cupped leaves with white ribs in a tightly bunched head.

# HEARTS OF PALM AND ALMOND SALAD

1/2 cup sliced almonds
1 tablespoon sugar
Rice vinegar
Canola oil
1 tablespoon chopped
  parsley
1/2 teaspoon minced garlic
1 head romaine lettuce,
  torn
2 to 4 sections hearts of
  palm, sliced
1 (11-ounce) can
  mandarin oranges,
  drained

Combine the almonds and sugar in a skillet. Cook over medium heat until the sugar is golden brown and coats the almonds, stirring constantly. Spread on a waxed paper-lined plate and chill until serving time.

Pour the vinegar to the vinegar line in a Good Seasons bottle. Add canola oil to the water line. Add the parsley and garlic and shake to mix well.

Combine the lettuce, hearts of palm and oranges in a salad bowl. Add the dressing and toss to coat well. Top with the almonds.

*Serves four*

# MIXED GREENS WITH FETA

**Raspberry Vinaigrette**
3 tablespoons olive oil
1/4 cup raspberry wine
  vinegar
1 1/2 teaspoons honey
Salt to taste

**Salad**
1/2 cup chopped walnuts
6 cups mixed salad greens
4 ounces feta cheese,
  crumbled
1/2 cup thinly sliced
  red onion

*For the dressing,* mix the olive oil, vinegar, honey and salt in a small bowl.

*For the salad,* spread the walnuts on a baking sheet. Toast at 350 degrees for 8 to 10 minutes or until golden brown.

Combine the walnuts with the salad greens, cheese and onion in a large bowl. Add the dressing and toss to coat.

NOTE: YOU MAY COMBINE THE ONION WITH A LITTLE OLIVE OIL IN A MICROWAVE-SAFE DISH AND MICROWAVE ON HIGH FOR 10 TO 20 SECONDS TO REMOVE THE SHARP TASTE IF DESIRED.

*Serves six*

# Rich and Charlie's Salad

1/4 cup olive oil
1/3 cup red wine vinegar
2 teaspoons sugar
Pepper to taste
1/2 cup grated Parmesan
    cheese
1 teaspoon minced garlic
1 (9-ounce) jar
    marinated artichoke
    hearts, chopped
1 small red onion,
    thinly sliced
1 (4-ounce) jar chopped
    pimentos
1 large head lettuce, torn

Combine the olive oil, vinegar, sugar and pepper in a bowl and mix well. Add the cheese, garlic, undrained artichokes, onion and pimentos and toss to coat well. Marinate at room temperature for 30 minutes.

Pour the marinated mixture over the lettuce in a large bowl. Chill until serving time. Toss to serve.

NOTE: YOU MAY SUBSTITUTE CANNED ARTICHOKE HEARTS FOR THE ARTICHOKES IN MARINADE AND INCREASE THE OLIVE OIL TO 1/2 CUP.

*Serves eight to ten*

# CORN AND TOMATO SALAD WITH BASIL

2 tablespoons olive oil
1 tablespoon finely
   chopped garlic
Kernels from 6 large ears
   white corn
1/2 cup julienned fresh
   basil leaves
5 plum tomatoes, seeded,
   chopped
3 tablespoons balsamic
   vinegar
3 tablespoons olive oil
Salt and pepper to taste

Heat 2 tablespoons olive oil in a heavy large skillet over medium-high heat. Add the garlic and sauté for 1 minute. Add the corn and sauté for 5 minutes or just until tender.

Combine the corn with half the basil in a large bowl and cool slightly, stirring occasionally. Add the remaining basil, tomatoes, vinegar and 3 tablespoons olive oil. Season with salt and pepper and toss to mix well. Chill for 3 to 8 hours.

*Serves six*

## Beverage Tips

### ORANGE MARGARITAS

Mix one 6-ounce can frozen orange juice concentrate with a juice can of tequila and 1/2 juice can of Triple Sec in a blender container. Add the juice of 1/2 orange and enough ice to fill the container and process until smooth. Dip the rims of the glasses into additional orange juice or water and then into sugar. Fill with the tequila mixture and garnish with orange wedges.

# Spinach Salad with Pecans and Feta

### Basil Vinaigrette

2$\frac{1}{2}$ tablespoons white wine vinegar  
$\frac{1}{4}$  cup vegetable oil  
1$\frac{1}{2}$ teaspoons sugar  
1    garlic clove, minced  
1    teaspoon dried basil  
$\frac{1}{4}$  teaspoon paprika  
$\frac{1}{8}$  teaspoon dry mustard

### Salad

$\frac{1}{3}$  cup pecans  
1    tablespoon butter  
Salt to taste  
1    large bunch spinach, torn  
$\frac{1}{2}$  cup crumbled feta cheese  
$\frac{3}{4}$  cup grated Parmesan cheese

*For the vinaigrette*, whisk the vinegar, oil, sugar, garlic, basil, paprika and dry mustard together in a small bowl.

*For the salad*, sauté the pecans in the butter in a skillet until golden brown. Drain on paper towels and sprinkle with salt.

Combine the spinach, pecans, feta cheese and Parmesan cheese in serving bowl. Add the dressing and toss to coat well.

*Serves four*

# SPINACH AND APPLE SALAD WITH BACON

**Vinegar and Oil Dressing**

1/4  cup vegetable oil
3    tablespoons red wine
     vinegar
1    teaspoon sugar
1/2  teaspoon prepared
     mustard
Salt and pepper to taste

**Salad**

5    slices bacon
1    cup slivered almonds
16   ounces fresh spinach,
     torn
2    red apples, chopped

*For the dressing,* combine the oil, vinegar, sugar, mustard, salt and pepper in a covered jar and shake until smooth. Chill in the refrigerator.

*For the salad,* cook the bacon in a skillet until crisp; drain the skillet, reserving 1 tablespoon of the drippings in the skillet. Crumble the bacon.

Add the almonds to the skillet and cook until golden brown. Combine the almonds with the spinach, apples and crumbled bacon in a bowl. Add the dressing and toss to serve.

*Serves four to six*

## Other Temptations

### BROWN DERBY DRESSING

Combine 3/4 cup red wine vinegar, 1 1/2 tablespoons lemon juice, 1 tablespoon Worcestershire sauce, 1 minced garlic clove, 1 teaspoon sugar, 1 teaspoon dry mustard, 3/4 teaspoon salt and 1 teaspoon pepper in a jar. Add 1 cup vegetable oil and 1 cup olive oil and cover. Shake to mix well and adjust the seasonings. Store, covered, in the refrigerator for up to 2 weeks. Shake again to serve.

# Mixed Greens and Mandarin Orange Salad

**Orange Dressing**
1 (11-ounce) can mandarin oranges
1/3 cup vegetable oil
1/4 cup white vinegar
1/4 cup sugar
1/2 teaspoon salt
1/2 teaspoon crushed red pepper

**Salad**
1 cup slivered almonds
6 tablespoons sugar
4 cups torn lettuce
4 cups torn spinach
1/4 cup chopped parsley
1 cup sliced celery

*For the dressing,* drain the mandarin oranges, reserving 2 tablespoons of the juice. Set aside the mandarin oranges for the salad. Combine the oil, vinegar, reserved mandarin orange juice, sugar, salt and red pepper in a covered jar and shake to mix well. Chill in the refrigerator.

*For the salad,* combine the almonds with the sugar in a heavy skillet. Cook over medium-low heat for 10 to 15 minutes or until the sugar melts and coats the almonds. Spread on foil and let stand until cool.

Combine the lettuce, spinach, parsley and celery in a large bowl. Break apart the almonds and add to the salad with the reserved mandarin oranges. Add the dressing and toss gently to coat well.

*Serves ten*

# Millennium Waldorf Salad

**Honey Yogurt Dressing**
2    teaspoons honey
1    cup plain nonfat yogurt
1/2  teaspoon grated
     orange zest
Salt to taste

**Salad**
1    Granny Smith apple
1    Red Delicious apple
1    pear
1    rib celery, sliced
1/4  cup golden raisins
1/4  cup toasted sliced
     almonds
3    tablespoons fresh
     orange juice
1    tablespoon fresh
     lemon juice
1    bunch spinach leaves

*For the dressing*, combine the honey, yogurt, orange zest and salt in a small bowl and mix well. Store in the refrigerator.

*For the salad*, chop the apples and pear into 1/2-inch pieces. Combine with the celery, raisins and almonds in a large bowl. Add the orange juice, lemon juice and 1/4 cup of the dressing.

Line the serving plates with spinach leaves and mound the salad in the center.

NOTE: NUTRITIONAL ANALYSIS INCLUDES THE ENTIRE AMOUNT OF THE DRESSING.

*Serves four*

## Tucson Times

### THE SONORAN DESERT

A desert is an arid place that receives on average less than ten inches of rain a year. With relative low humidity and little to no cloud cover, daytime temperatures soar while nights cool drastically resulting in temperature swings that are often greater than 30 degrees.

# WALNUT AND GORGONZOLA SALAD

**Orange Mustard Vinaigrette**
- 1/4  cup orange juice
- 1/4  cup olive oil
- 2  tablespoons walnut oil
- 2  teaspoons Dijon
  mustard

**Salad**
- 1  cup walnuts
- 1  tablespoon butter
- Salt to taste
- 16  ounces mixed greens
- 3/4  cup crumbled
  Gorgonzola cheese
- 1 1/2 cup drained mandarin
  oranges

*For the vinaigrette*, whisk together the orange juice, olive oil, walnut oil and Dijon mustard in a small bowl.

*For the salad*, toast the walnuts with the butter in a skillet, stirring to coat well. Drain on paper towels and sprinkle with salt.

Combine the walnuts with the mixed greens in a bowl. Add the vinaigrette and toss to coat well. Spoon onto serving plates and sprinkle with the cheese. Arrange the oranges around the greens.

*Serves four*

## Cooking Tips

### ABOUT NUTS

Nuts are better for you than they are cracked up to be. They contain mostly monounsaturated fat, which doesn't raise blood cholesterol levels. They are also a good source of protein and vitamin E. At least 70 percent of their calories, however, are from fat, with Macadamia nuts having the most. One-fourth cup of Macadamias has 205 calories and 22 fat grams. The least fatty are pistachios and peanuts with 14 grams, and cashews with 13 grams. Almonds have 15 grams, black walnuts have 16, pine nuts 17, English walnuts and hazelnuts 18, and pecans and Brazil nuts 19.

# HONEY CREAM DRESSING

1/2 cup sesame seeds
1 tablespoon butter
3 ounces cream cheese,
    softened
1/4 cup sour cream
2 tablespoons honey
Salt to taste
2 tablespoons (about)
    milk or mandarin
    orange juice

Spread the sesame seeds on a baking sheet and dot with the butter. Roast until golden brown, stirring frequently.

Combine the cream cheese, sour cream, honey and salt in a mixing bowl and beat until smooth. Add the milk and sesame seeds and mix well. Store in the refrigerator.

Serve over a salad of spinach and mandarin oranges. Add chicken for a main dish salad.

*Makes one cup*

# CREAMY BLACK PEPPER DRESSING

1/4 vegetable bouillon cube
2 tablespoons hot water
1/2 cup creamy tofu,
    drained
1 small garlic clove,
    minced
1 tablespoon grated
    Romano cheese
1 tablespoon fresh
    lemon juice
1 teaspoon canola oil
1/4 teaspoon sugar
1/2 teaspoon black
    peppercorns
Salt to taste

Dissolve the bouillon in the hot water in a blender container. Add the tofu, garlic, cheese, lemon juice, canola oil, sugar and peppercorns and process until smooth. Season with salt. Chill for 1 hour to 3 days; dressing will thicken as it stands. Stir to serve.

*Serves six*

# Hearty
# Temptations

## MEATS

# Rodeo Barbecue

*Kicked off with the largest non-mechanized parade in the world, La Fiesta de los Vaqueros (Festival of Cowboys) is America's largest outdoor winter rodeo and the oldest in the Southwest. The rodeo, with shows of calf roping, bareback riding, steer wrestling, and more, is just one of many celebrations held during rodeo week. At least one of those rodeo days should end with your boots kicked off and a plateful of this barbecue meal.*

## Menu

Chicken Tikka

Bass Ale Shrimp

Mustard-Glazed Spareribs

Fiesta Pasta Salad

Citrus Bean Salad

New England Apple Pie

# Austrian Beef Strudel

3   tablespoons unsalted
    butter or olive oil
1   large onion, finely
    chopped
1   pound ground beef
1   teaspoon minced garlic
3   tablespoons chopped
    fresh parsley
3   tablespoons chopped
    fresh dill
1   teaspoon dried oregano
1   teaspoon ground
    cinnamon
1/2 teaspoon ground
    allspice or grated
    nutmeg
1   egg
1/4 cup fine dry bread
    crumbs
Salt and freshly ground
    pepper to taste
12  sheets frozen phyllo
    pastry, thawed
1/2 cup (1 stick) unsalted
    butter, melted

Melt 3 tablespoons butter in a large skillet over medium heat. Add the onion and sauté for 8 to 10 minutes or until tender. Add the ground beef, garlic, parsley, dill, oregano, cinnamon and allspice. Sauté for 10 minutes or until the beef is cooked through and crumbly, stirring occasionally with a wooden spoon; drain. Spoon into a bowl and cool slightly. Add the egg, bread crumbs, salt and pepper and mix well. Cool for 20 minutes longer.

Layer 6 sheets of phyllo pastry on a work surface with the long side at the bottom, brushing each sheet with some of the melted butter. Spoon half the beef mixture in a strip along the nearest edge, leaving a 1-inch border. Fold in the pastry ends and roll to enclose the filling. Repeat the process with the remaining phyllo pastry and beef sauce.

Place the rolls on a buttered baking sheet; brush with the remaining melted butter. Bake at 350 degrees for 40 minutes or until golden brown. Cut into 1/2-inch slices to serve.

*Serves six*

# BAKED POBLANO CHILE AND
# BEEF CASSEROLE

1   *pound ground beef*
2   *yellow squash, shredded or sliced*
2   *zucchini, shredded or sliced*
1   *cup chopped roasted poblano chiles, or 1 (4-ounce) can chopped green chiles*
1   *small onion, chopped*
1   *cup shredded Cheddar cheese*
1   *tablespoon butter*
1   *egg, beaten*

Brown the ground beef in a skillet, stirring until crumbly; drain. Reserve some of the yellow squash and zucchini for the top layer.

Layer the remaining squash, chiles, onion, cheese and ground beef 1/2 at a time in a baking dish sprayed with nonstick cooking spray.

Dot with the butter and pour the egg over the layers. Bake at 350 degrees for 45 to 60 minutes or until the casserole is bubbly and the ground beef is cooked through.

*Serves four to six*

## *Tucson Times*

### DAVIS-MONTHAN AIR BASE

Colonel Charles Lindbergh, following his successful solo flight across the Atlantic Ocean, came to Tucson in 1927 to dedicate the local airfield as an Army Signal Corps base. It was the largest municipal airport in the United States at the time and the first to become a military base, named for two Tucson military aviators. The field served both military and commercial flights for ten years after becoming an Army Signal Corps base. Amelia Earhart, Wiley Post, and James Dolittle all landed at the base.

# FIREHOUSE CHILI

1¹/2 to 2 pounds
    ground beef
1   cup chopped onion
3 to 5 garlic cloves, minced
1   (16-ounce) can
    kidney beans
1   (16-ounce) can
    tomatoes, chopped
2   (15-ounce) cans
    tomato sauce
12  ounces fresh or canned
    green chiles, seeded,
    chopped
1 to 2 tablespoons sugar
1   teaspoon
    Worcestershire sauce
Hot pepper sauce to taste
2   bay leaves
2 to 3 tablespoons chili
    powder
3   tablespoons ground
    cumin
¹/2  teaspoon onion powder
¹/2  teaspoon dried basil
¹/2  teaspoon Italian
    seasoning
1   teaspoon salt
¹/2  teaspoon cayenne
    pepper
¹/2  teaspoon crushed red
    pepper flakes
1   teaspoon black pepper

Brown the ground beef with the onion and garlic in a large saucepan, stirring until the ground beef is crumbly; drain. Add the beans, tomatoes, tomato sauce, chiles, sugar, Worcestershire sauce, hot pepper sauce, bay leaves, chili powder, cumin, onion powder, basil, Italian seasoning, salt, cayenne pepper, crushed red pepper and black pepper; mix well.

Reduce the heat and simmer, covered for 1 hour; discard the bay leaves. Serve over rice or pasta if desired.

NOTE: THIS DISH CAN BE PREPARED IN A SLOW COOKER IF DESIRED.

*Serves six to eight*

# SONORAN STEW

2 pounds ground beef
1 large onion, chopped
3/4 cup water
1 (28-ounce) can
   tomatoes, chopped
1 (16-ounce) package
   frozen corn
3 medium potatoes,
   peeled, chopped
1 cup salsa
1/2 teaspoon garlic powder,
   or 1 chopped
   garlic clove
1 teaspoon ground cumin
1 teaspoon salt
1/2 teaspoon pepper
2 tablespoons flour
1/4 cup water

Brown the ground beef with the onion in a heavy saucepan, stirring until the ground beef is crumbly; drain. Add 3/4 cup water, undrained tomatoes, corn, potatoes, salsa, garlic powder, cumin, salt and pepper. Bring to a boil and reduce the heat. Simmer, covered, for 1 1/2 hours.

Blend the flour with 1/4 cup water in a small bowl. Stir into the stew. Cook until slightly thickened, stirring constantly. Garnish the servings with shredded cheese and/or sour cream.

NOTE: OMIT THE SALT TO REDUCE THE SODIUM IN THIS STEW.

Serves six

## Beverage Tips

### DECANTING WINE

Red wines may have sediment that begins to develop eight years after bottling. They will benefit from decanting by pouring into a glass carafe or decanter to allow the oxygen from the air to combine with the wine and release the wine's flavor. This will allow the sediment to settle.

# SWEDISH MEATBALLS

3/4 cup bread crumbs
3/4 cup hot water
1 pound ground beef
8 ounces ground pork
1 small red onion, grated
1 egg
1/2 teaspoon sugar
1 teaspoon ground allspice
1/2 teaspoon garlic powder
1 teaspoon salt
1/2 teaspoon white pepper
2 tablespoons butter or margarine, melted
2 tablespoons flour
2 tablespoons butter, melted
2 cups milk
Salt to taste

Soak the bread crumbs in the hot water in a large bowl. Add the ground beef, ground pork, onion, egg, sugar, allspice, garlic powder, 1 teaspoon salt and white pepper and mix well. Shape into small balls with hands dipped into cold water.

Fry the meatballs 8 to 10 at a time in 2 tablespoons melted butter in a skillet over medium heat, shaking the skillet to brown evenly; drain.

Blend the flour into 2 tablespoons melted butter in a saucepan. Cook until bubbly, stirring constantly. Stir in the milk gradually. Add salt to taste. Cook until thickened, stirring constantly. Add the meatballs and cook until heated through. Serve with mashed potatoes.

*Serves eight*

## Other Temptations

### CREAM GRAVY

Sauté 1/2 cup chopped onion in 1/4 cup pan drippings or unsalted butter in a medium saucepan over low heat for 3 minutes. Whisk in 1/4 cup flour and cook for 2 to 3 minutes or until smooth. Add 2 1/4 cups milk and 2 bouillon cubes. Bring to a boil and reduce the heat, stirring constantly. Cook for 5 minutes or until thickened, stirring constantly. Strain if necessary and season with salt and pepper. Add 1 teaspoon crumbled dried sage to chicken gravy.

# BULGOGI

1    pound sirloin steak,
     frozen
$^1/4$  cup minced onion
2    teaspoons minced garlic
$^1/4$  cup soy sauce
2    tablespoons sugar
Red pepper to taste
1    teaspoon black pepper
2    tablespoons toasted
     sesame seeds
2    tablespoons
     sesame oil

Slice the sirloin $^1/4$ inch thick. Combine the slices with the onion, garlic, soy sauce, sugar, red pepper, black pepper, sesame seeds and sesame oil in a bowl and mix to coat well. Marinate in the refrigerator for 2 to 3 hours.

Grill on a very hot grill for 1 minute on each side. Serve with hot cooked rice.

*Serves four*

# SHREDDED BEEF

3 to 5 pounds chuck roast
2    cups water
1    tablespoon
     Worcestershire sauce
2    teaspoons garlic powder
1    teaspoon dry mustard
1    teaspoon salt
1    teaspoon pepper

Combine the beef, water, Worcestershire sauce, garlic powder, dry mustard, salt and pepper in a slow cooker. Cook on Low for 12 hours. Remove the beef and shred. Serve with the cooking juices on hard rolls.

*Serves twelve*

# Pastel de Choclo

3    (10-ounce) packages
     frozen corn or corn
     kernels cut from
     12 ears
1/4  cup milk
1    teaspoon chopped
     fresh basil
1    egg
1    pound sirloin steak
1    medium onion, chopped
1    tablespoon olive oil
Tabasco sauce to taste
2    tablespoons curry
     powder
Salt and pepper to taste
2    tablespoons sugar

Combine the corn, milk and basil in a saucepan. Simmer for 20 minutes or until thickened. Cool to room temperature. Add some of the mixture to the egg. Add the egg to the saucepan and mix well.

Cut the steak into bite-size pieces. Sauté the onion in the olive oil in a skillet for 1 minute. Add the steak, Tabasco sauce, curry powder, salt and pepper. Cook for 10 minutes or until the steak is brown.

Spread the steak mixture in a baking dish. Spread the corn mixture over the steak and sprinkle with the sugar. Bake at 350 degrees for 30 minutes or until golden brown.

Serves four

# STEAK AU POIVRE

3 tablespoons peppercorns
2 (10-ounce) New York
  strip steaks
1 teaspoon kosher salt or
  iodized salt
¹/4 cup vegetable oil
¹/3 cup cognac

Crush the peppercorns and press into both sides of the steaks. Let stand for 10 minutes; pound lightly with a meat mallet. Sprinkle half the salt on 1 side of the steaks.

Cook the steaks salt side down in the heated oil in a skillet over high heat for 2 to 3 minutes or until seared, shaking to prevent sticking. Sprinkle with the remaining salt and turn the steaks. Cook for 2 to 3 minutes.

Reduce the heat and cook the steaks for 2 minutes longer on each side. Remove to a heated platter. Stir the cognac into the skillet and ignite. Let flame subside and pour over the steaks. Serve immediately.

*Serves two*

---

## Cooking Tips

### MEXICAN DISHES

Sopapillas probably developed from Navajo fry bread. Although the frying technique is different, the dough is similar. The Navajo originally cooked the bread on the end of a green pinion twig, the bread is now cooked in lard in cast-iron pots and then heated over open fires.

Quesadillas are wheat tortillas covered with Monterey Jack cheese and jalapeño chiles, folded, and quickly grilled.

The word enchilada actually means to cover with chiles. Enchiladas originated as corn tortillas dipped in chiles. They now include a variety of fillings, such as cheese or chicken, wrapped in a corn tortilla, and smothered in a red chile sauce.

# SPICED BEEF TENDERLOIN WITH MANGO SALSA

## Mango Salsa

1/2   cup jalapeño jelly
3   tablespoons fresh lime juice
2¹/2 cups chopped mangoes
1¹/4 cups chopped red bell peppers
3/4   cup chopped red onion
1/3   cup chopped fresh cilantro
1   jalapeño chile, minced
Salt and pepper to taste

## Spiced Steaks

1   tablespoon sugar
1   tablespoon paprika
1   tablespoon cinnamon
1   tablespoon ground coriander
1¹/2 teaspoons salt
1/2   teaspoon cayenne pepper
12   (4-ounce) beef tenderloin steaks
Olive oil

*For the salsa,* whisk the jelly and lime juice together in a large bowl. Add the mangoes, bell peppers, onion, cilantro and chile. Season to taste with salt and pepper. Chill for up to 2 hours in the refrigerator.

*For the beef,* mix the sugar, paprika, cinnamon, coriander, salt and cayenne pepper in a small bowl. Brush the steaks with olive oil and sprinkle 1/2 teaspoon of the mixture on each side. Grill over medium-hot coals for 2 minutes for medium-rare, or until done to taste. Serve with the salsa.

*Serves six*

# CABERNET AND THYME FILLETS OF BEEF

2   cups cabernet
    sauvignon or other
    dry red wine
1   bay leaf
6   peppercorns, crushed
2   garlic cloves, crushed
2   whole cloves
1   allspice berry, crushed
2   sprigs fresh thyme
2   (3-inch) strips
    orange zest
4   (8-ounce) beef fillets,
    1¹/₂ inches thick
1   cup beef stock
Kosher salt to taste
2 to 4 tablespoons
    unsalted butter

Bring the wine to a simmer in a small saucepan over medium heat. Add the bay leaf, peppercorns, garlic, cloves, allspice, thyme and orange zest. Simmer for 15 minutes; let stand until completely cool. Pour the wine mixture over the fillets in a shallow dish. Marinate, covered, at room temperature for up to 4 hours, or in the refrigerator for up to 12 hours.

Bring the beef stock to a boil in a small saucepan and cook for 20 minutes or until reduced by half. Remove the beef from the marinade and reserve the marinade. Pat the beef dry and sprinkle with kosher salt. Pan-broil in a heavy skillet over high heat for 3 minutes on each side for rare, or until done to taste. Remove to a warm platter.

Strain 1 cup of the reserved marinade into the skillet, stirring to deglaze the bottom. Cook until reduced by half. Add the reduced beef stock and cook until reduced again by half. Stir in the butter and cook just until thickened and smooth. Spoon over the fillets.

*Serves four*

---

## About Thyme

### THYME TO CHOOSE

There are many varieties of thyme. Wild French thyme, or serpolet, grown mostly in Provence gives the cooking of the region its distinctive flavor. Lemon thyme has a citrus-like perfume and is excellent as an herb tea; it can be used in both sweet and savory dishes. Golden thyme has a woody stem and pale lilac blooms in the summer. Its leaves are oval, green, and covered with fine hairs.

# INDIVIDUAL BEEF WELLINGTON

8   (5- to 6-ounce) beef
    fillets
2   tablespoons
    vegetable oil
1   teaspoon salt
1/2 teaspoon pepper
8   frozen puff pastry
    shells, thawed
4   ounces pâté de foie gras
1   egg white, at room
    temperature
1   teaspoon water

Place the fillets in the freezer for 20 minutes. Brush with the oil and place in a heated skillet. Sear for 3 minutes on each side. Remove from the skillet, sprinkle with the salt and pepper and place in the refrigerator for 20 minutes.

Place the pastry shells on waxed paper and sprinkle the shells and rolling pin lightly with flour. Roll the shells 1/8 inch thick.

Shape the pâté into 8 small disks and place 1 on each pastry. Place the fillets on the pâté and fold the pastry to enclose completely, pressing to seal.

Place sealed side down 1 inch apart on a baking sheet and make a small hole in the center of each pastry. Cut designs from remaining pastry scraps and arrange on the tops.

Beat the egg white with the water in a cup and brush over the pastry. Bake in the upper third of a 450-degree oven for 10 minutes for rare, for 12 minutes for medium-rare or for 15 minutes for medium. Place under the broiler for 2 to 3 minutes if necessary to brown the crust. Serve with Classic Béarnaise Sauce (page 48).

NOTE: WELLINGTONS CAN BE PREPARED, COVERED WITH FOIL AND PLACED IN THE REFRIGERATOR FOR 8 HOURS OR LONGER. DO NOT BAKE ON A NONSTICK BAKING SHEET.

*Serves eight*

# OLD MAIN

On October 1, 1891, the first university in all of Arizona opened its doors. Thirty-two
students entered Old Main that day to begin the semester. Although few of the buildings erected
in the university's early days still stand, Old Main has remained a visual and spiritual
center of the campus. To honor the students lost in World War I, a fountain was erected in front
of Old Main. Over the past century, the University of Arizona has seen much growth and recognition.
It now boasts 35,000 students and is one of the premier research universities in the nation.

# GOURMET STROGANOFF

| | |
|---|---|
| 1 | *pound beef tenderloin* |
| 1/8 | *teaspoon minced garlic* |
| 2 | *teaspoons Worcestershire sauce* |
| 1 | *small bay leaf, crumbled* |
| *Paprika to taste* | |
| 1 | *teaspoon seasoned salt* |
| 1/4 | *teaspoon pepper* |
| 1 | *teaspoon butter* |
| 1 1/4 | *cups finely chopped onions* |
| 2 | *teaspoons butter* |
| 1/2 | *cup sliced mushrooms* |
| 1 | *tablespoon cornstarch* |
| 1/4 | *cup tomato juice* |
| 1/2 | *cup sour cream* |
| 1/4 | *cup buttermilk* |

Cut the beef into thin strips. Toss with the garlic, Worcestershire sauce, bay leaf, paprika, seasoned salt and pepper in a bowl. Sauté in 1 teaspoon butter in a large skillet until the beef is nearly cooked through.

Sauté the onions in 2 teaspoons butter in a small skillet until light brown. Add to the beef and cook for several minutes. Stir in the mushrooms.

Blend the cornstarch into the tomato juice in a small bowl. Add to the beef mixture. Simmer for 5 minutes or until thickened, stirring constantly.

Mix the sour cream and buttermilk in a small bowl. Add to the beef mixture. Cook just until heated through; do not allow to boil. Serve over buttered noodles or rice pilaf.

*Serves four to six*

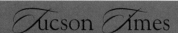

## Tucson Times

### WAR MEMORIAL

General John J. Pershing, commander of the American Expeditionary Force in World War I, dedicated the fountain west of Old Main on the University of Arizona campus in 1920 as a memorial for students who had died in the war. Harry Berger, whose son did not return from the war, donated funds for the memorial.

# SUMATRAN BEEF

3 pounds beef chuck or
   other stewing beef
Vegetable oil for frying
4 to 5 cups chopped onions
3 tablespoons
   vegetable oil
3 tablespoons grated
   gingerroot
2 tablespoons
   minced garlic
1 teaspoon minced
   jalapeño chile, or
   to taste
1 teaspoon ground
   turmeric
2 tablespoons ground
   coriander
2 bay leaves
2 long strips lemon zest,
   or 2 stalks fresh lemon
   grass, crushed and cut
   into 3-inch pieces
3 cups coconut milk
2 cups beef stock
Salt and freshly ground
   pepper to taste

Cut the beef into $1^{1}/4$-inch cubes. Pour enough oil into a skillet to just cover the bottom and heat over high heat. Add the beef in batches and fry for 10 to 15 minutes or until brown on all sides; remove with a slotted spoon.

Sauté the onions in 3 tablespoons heated oil in a large heavy saucepan over medium heat for 10 to 15 minutes or until tender and translucent. Add the gingerroot, garlic, chile, turmeric, coriander, bay leaves and lemon zest and cook for 5 minutes longer.

Add the beef to the saucepan with the coconut milk and beef stock. Simmer, covered, for 3 hours or until the beef is very tender. Season with salt and pepper; discard the bay leaves and lemon zest or lemon grass.

Serves six

# MESQUITE-GRILLED LAMB CHOPS

1/4  cup (1/2 stick) butter or
     margarine, melted
3    tablespoons fresh
     lemon juice
4    garlic cloves, crushed
     or minced
1/2  teaspoon chopped fresh
     rosemary
6    (1 1/2-inch) lamb rib or
     loin chops

Combine the melted butter, lemon juice, garlic and rosemary in a small bowl and mix well.

Place the lamb chops on a rack 4 to 6 inches above a bed of hot mesquite wood coals. Grill for 10 to 15 minutes for medium-rare or until done to taste, turning once and basting frequently with the butter mixture. Garnish with fresh rosemary sprigs.

NOTE: THE MESQUITE FIRE IS HOT ENOUGH WHEN YOU CAN HOLD YOUR HAND AT RACK LEVEL FOR NO MORE THAN 2 TO 3 SECONDS.

*Serves six*

## Cooking Tips

### STORING GARLIC

Prevent garlic cloves from drying out by storing them in a bottle of cooking oil. After the garlic is used, the garlic-flavored oil can also be used for cooking and in salads. Remember to remove the green sprout from the center of a garlic clove to eliminate a bitter taste.

# MUSTARD-GLAZED SPARERIBS

1   small onion, chopped
2   tablespoons
    vegetable oil
1   cup honey
1   cup Dijon mustard
1/2 cup cider vinegar
1   teaspoon ground cloves
1/2 teaspoon salt
6   pounds (about) baby
    back rib sections
Salt and freshly ground
    pepper to taste

Sauté the onion in the heated oil in a saucepan over medium heat for 5 minutes or until tender. Add the honey, mustard, vinegar, cloves and 1/2 teaspoon salt and mix well. Bring to a boil and reduce the heat. Simmer for 5 minutes, stirring occasionally.

Sprinkle the ribs generously on both sides with salt and pepper. Place on an oiled grill rack 4 to 6 inches above a heated grill with a cover. Cover the grill and open the vents halfway. Grill for 40 minutes, turning once, adding coals if necessary to maintain an even heat.

Brush the ribs with the mustard mixture and grill, covered, for 10 minutes. Turn the ribs and brush again with the mustard mixture. Grill for 10 minutes longer.

Cut the ribs into single-rib servings. Heat the remaining basting sauce until bubbly. Serve with the ribs.

*Serves six*

# CRANBERRY-GLAZED PORK ROAST

2     teaspoons cornstarch
2     tablespoons
      orange juice
2     tablespoons dry sherry
1     (16-ounce) can whole
      cranberry sauce
$1/2$   teaspoon grated
      orange zest
$1/4$   teaspoon cinnamon
$1/8$   teaspoon salt
1     (4-pound) boneless
      pork loin roast

Blend the cornstarch into the orange juice and sherry in a small saucepan. Add the cranberry sauce, orange zest, cinnamon and salt and mix well. Cook over medium heat until thickened, stirring constantly.

Place the roast in a shallow roasting pan and insert a meat thermometer into the thickest portion. Roast at 325 degrees for 45 minutes. Spoon $1/2$ cup of the cranberry glaze over the roast. Roast for 30 to 45 minutes longer or to 155 to 160 degrees on the meat thermometer. Let stand for 10 minutes before slicing. Serve with the remaining cranberry glaze.

*Serves twelve*

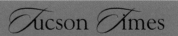

## "A" MOUNTAIN

Sentinel Peak is known to Tucsonans as "A" mountain because of the large "A" on the face of the peak. It has been whitewashed every year since 1915 by the freshmen students of the University of Arizona as part of the annual homecoming events.

# SEED-ENCRUSTED PORK ROAST

1 to 2 teaspoons mixed
    peppercorns
2    teaspoons coriander
    seeds
1    tablespoon fennel seeds
2    teaspoons cumin seeds
1    tablespoon dried
    onion flakes
6    tablespoons butter,
    softened
$1/4$  cup flour
Salt to taste
1    ($4^1/2$-pound)
    pork roast
$1/4$  cup flour
$1^3/4$ cups chicken broth
1    cup (about) water
1    tablespoon red wine
    vinegar

Combine the peppercorns, coriander seeds, fennel seeds, cumin seeds and onion flakes in a nonstick skillet. Cook over medium heat for 2 to 3 minutes or until toasted, stirring constantly. Grind the seed mixture coarsely.

Mix the butter and 1/4 cup flour to form a paste in a small bowl. Add the seed mixture and salt to taste and mix well. Press firmly over the top of the roast.

Place the pork in a roasting pan. Roast at 450 degrees for 20 minutes. Reduce the oven temperature to 325 degrees and roast for 1 1/2 hours longer.

Remove the roast to a platter; drain the roasting pan, pouring 1/4 to 1/3 cup of the drippings into a saucepan. Stir in 1/4 cup flour. Cook for 3 minutes or until bubbly and smooth, stirring constantly. Whisk in the chicken broth and water. Bring to a boil, add the vinegar and correct the seasonings, stirring constantly. Serve with the roast. Garnish with rosemary sprigs. Serve with poblano chiles stuffed with black beans and goat cheese or acorn halves stuffed with saffron-scented pearl onions.

*Serves eight*

# TUSCAN TENDERLOIN

**Pork**

| | |
|---|---|
| 1 | (12-ounce) pork tenderloin |
| Salt to taste | |
| 1/2 | cup cooked white beans |
| 1 | green onion, chopped |
| 1/4 | cup chopped roasted red bell pepper |

**Balsamic Caper Marinade**

| | |
|---|---|
| 1/4 | cup olive oil |
| 2 | tablespoons balsamic vinegar |
| 1 | tablespoon water |
| 1 | garlic clove, minced |
| 1 | tablespoon chopped fresh basil |
| 1 | tablespoon dried currants |
| 2 | tablespoons drained capers |
| 1/2 | teaspoon coarsely ground pepper |

*For the pork,* slice down the center of the tenderloin, cutting to but not through the bottom. Spread the halves and sprinkle with salt. Cover with plastic wrap and pound 1/4 inch thick with the flat side of a meat mallet.

Combine the beans, green onion and bell pepper in a bowl. Spread over the tenderloin, leaving a 1/4-inch edge. Roll up from the narrow side to enclose the filling; secure with wooden picks. Place seam side down on a rack in a shallow roasting pan.

Roast at 325 degrees for 45 minutes or until the juices run clear. Cover and let stand for 15 minutes. Cut into 12 slices and arrange the slices on a platter.

*For the marinade,* combine the olive oil, vinegar, water, garlic, basil, currants, capers and pepper in a bowl.

Spoon the marinade over the pork. Marinate, covered, in the refrigerator for 4 to 6 hours. Let stand at room temperature for 30 minutes before serving.

*To serve,* arrange the slices on a lettuce-lined plate. Garnish with chive stems and currants or small grapes.

*Serves four*

# CARAMELIZED PORK OVER LETTUCE

2  tablespoons sugar
2  tablespoons water
2  tablespoons fish sauce
1 1/2  pounds boneless
    pork loin
1  teaspoon vegetable oil
1  (10-ounce) can
    reduced-sodium
    chicken broth
1  (3-inch) cinnamon
    stick
1/4  teaspoon pepper
2  cups (2-inch) green
    onion pieces
1/2  teaspoon vegetable oil
6  cups shredded
    romaine lettuce
1/4  cup thinly sliced
    fresh basil
1/4  cup minced fresh
    cilantro
1/4  cup rice vinegar

Sprinkle the sugar in a small heavy saucepan. Cook over medium heat for 5 minutes to caramelize; do not stir. Stir in the water and fish sauce carefully.

Cut the pork into 1-inch cubes. Heat 1 teaspoon oil in a large skillet coated with nonstick cooking spray. Add the pork and cook for 4 minutes or until browned on all sides; remove with a slotted spoon.

Add the chicken broth to the skillet, stirring to deglaze. Return the pork to the skillet. Add the caramelized sugar mixture, cinnamon stick and pepper and bring to a boil. Reduce the heat and simmer, covered for 1 1/2 hours or until the pork is very tender. Remove to a bowl and keep warm, discarding the cinnamon stick.

Sauté the green onions in 1/2 teaspoon oil in a small skillet. Add to the pork and mix well. Combine the lettuce, basil and cilantro in a large bowl. Add the vinegar and toss to coat well. Spoon onto serving plates. Top with the pork mixture.

*Serves six*

## Other Temptations

### HONEY-SESAME PORK TENDERLOIN

Combine a 12-ounce pork tenderloin with a mixture of 1/4 cup soy sauce, 2 sliced garlic cloves and a thinly sliced 2-inch piece of gingerroot in a bowl. Marinate in the refrigerator for 1 hour; drain and pat dry. Roll the pork in 1/4 cup honey and then in 1 cup sesame seeds, coating well. Roast at 400 degrees for 20 minutes.

# FRUITED PORK CHOPS

2 tablespoons
  vegetable oil
6 lean pork chops
2 garlic cloves, minced
1 medium onion, chopped
1/2 cup sliced celery
1 (16-ounce) can juice-
  pack pineapple chunks
6 pitted prunes, cut
  into halves
6 dried apricots, cut
  into halves
2 tablespoons soy sauce
2 tablespoons minced
  celery leaves
1/2 teaspoon marjoram
Garlic powder to taste
Salt and pepper to taste

Heat the oil to 350 degrees in a skillet. Add the pork chops and cook until brown on both sides. Add the garlic and sauté for 2 minutes. Add the onion and celery and sauté for 3 to 5 minutes or until tender.

Add the undrained pineapple chunks, prunes, apricots, soy sauce, celery leaves, marjoram, garlic powder, salt and pepper and mix gently. Simmer, covered, for 15 to 20 minutes, adding water as needed.

*Serves six*

## Other Temptations

### BLACK CURRANT PORK

Sprinkle 6 center-cut pork chops with salt and pepper and brown on both sides in a nonstick skillet. Add a mixture of 1/4 cup black currant preserves and 1 1/2 tablespoons Dijon mustard. Reduce the heat and cook, covered, for 20 minutes or until cooked through. Remove the pork chops and keep warm in the oven; drain the skillet. Add 1/3 cup rice wine vinegar to the skillet and stir to deglaze the bottom. Cook until reduced by one third and pour over the pork chops to serve.

# BROILED VEAL LOIN CHOPS WITH
# TARRAGON SHERRY CREAM

### Tarragon Sherry Cream

6 tablespoons unsalted
butter
6 to 8 shallots, chopped
12 ounces mushrooms,
sliced 1/4 inch thick
2 tablespoons minced
fresh tarragon, or
1 tablespoon dried
tarragon
1/2 cup dry white wine
1 cup heavy cream
Salt and pepper to taste

### Veal Chops

6 (12-ounce) veal chops
Olive oil
Salt and freshly ground
pepper to taste

*For the sauce*, melt the butter in a sauté pan over medium heat. Add the shallots and sauté for 5 minutes or until tender. Increase the heat and add the mushrooms. Sauté for 1 to 2 minutes or until the mushrooms are tender and give off some of their moisture. Add the tarragon, wine and cream and cook until slightly reduced. Season with salt and pepper and keep warm.

*For the veal*, brush the chops lightly with olive oil and sprinkle with salt and pepper. Broil or grill for 4 minutes on each side or until done to taste, turning once.

*To serve*, place the chops on serving plates and spoon the sauce over the top.

*Serves six*

# Savory Temptations

## POULTRY

# Holiday Dinner Party

*Winterhaven is an established neighborhood whose residents decorate
their homes during the holiday season with lavish and creative
light displays. This popular event usually sees bumper-to-bumper traffic,
so walking tours or rides in horse-drawn carriages have become a
more relaxed method of seeing the glowing spectacle. Like the Winterhaven
tours, this meal can be enjoyed either as a sit-down affair or buffet style.*

## Menu

Currant and Cranberry Brie

Chicken Breasts Stuffed with
Goat Cheese and Basil

Mashed Potatoes with Caramelized
Onions

Asparagus with Mushrooms
and Fresh Cilantro

Macadamia-Crusted Pear Torte

Spiced Wine

# BROILED CHICKEN WITH MUSHROOMS

2   garlic cloves, crushed
1/4  cup (1/2 stick) butter
2   (2-pound) chickens,
    split into halves
Lemon juice
38  large fresh mushrooms,
    or 2 drained (8-ounce)
    cans mushrooms
2   teaspoons dried
    marjoram
Grated nutmeg to taste
1/2  teaspoon salt
1/4  cup (1/2 stick) butter

Combine the garlic with 1/4 cup butter in a saucepan and cook until the butter melts. Brush the chickens with lemon juice. Place the chicken skin side down on a rack in a broiler pan and brush generously with the garlic butter.

Broil the chicken for 27 minutes or until golden brown, turning after 12 minutes and basting frequently with the garlic butter. Remove the rack from the broiler pan and place the chicken directly in the pan; baste again. Reduce the oven temperature to 300 degrees.

Sauté the mushrooms with the marjoram, nutmeg and salt in 1/4 cup butter in a skillet over low heat for 4 minutes. Spoon over the chicken. Roast at 300 degrees for 20 to 30 minutes or until cooked through.

*Serves four*

# ROSEMARY AND GARLIC BAKED CHICKEN

8   fresh rosemary sprigs,
    cut into pieces
10  garlic cloves,
    thinly sliced
1   (4-pound) chicken,
    cut into 8 pieces
2   tablespoons olive oil
Salt and pepper to taste
Juice of 1 lemon
1   lemon, sliced

Place several small rosemary pieces and garlic slices under the skin of each chicken piece. Arrange the chicken in a 9 × 13-inch baking pan and drizzle with the olive oil. Turn the chicken to coat evenly with the oil and season with salt and pepper. Drizzle with the lemon juice and arrange the lemon slices and remaining rosemary and garlic under and around the chicken.

Bake at 325 degrees for 55 minutes or just until cooked through. Broil for 5 minutes or until golden brown.

*Serves four*

# CHICKEN CHILAQUILES

2 dried ancho chiles
2 tomatoes, chopped
3 eggs
1 cup beer
1 cup sour cream
Salt and pepper to taste
12 tortilla chips
2 chicken breasts,
   poached, shredded
1²/3 cups shredded
   Cheddar cheese

Cut the chiles into halves lengthwise, discarding the stems, seeds and membranes. Place in an ungreased skillet and cook for 3 minutes or until roasted. Combine with water to cover in a bowl and let stand for 5 minutes; drain.

Combine the chiles with the tomatoes, eggs, beer, sour cream, salt and pepper in a food processor or blender container and process until smooth.

Layer the tortilla chips and chicken in a 9 × 13-inch baking dish. Spread the chile mixture over the layers and sprinkle with the cheese. Bake at 400 degrees for 30 minutes or until bubbly.

*Serves six*

## Beverage Tips

### AGAVE TEQUILA

In the well at the heart of the giant agave, or century plant, is a thick yellow liquid or honey. When fermented and then refined, it becomes mescal and tequila.

# Coq au Vin Western Style

4   skinless chicken breasts
1   tablespoon olive oil
1   tablespoon butter
2   tablespoons minced
    garlic
Salt and pepper to taste
2   cups red wine
1 to 2 cups reduced-sodium
    chicken broth
2   cups sliced carrots
Sliced mushrooms
1   medium onion, chopped
2   green chiles, chopped
1   tablespoon olive oil
1   tablespoon butter
2   tablespoons flour

Brown the chicken lightly in 1 tablespoon olive oil and 1 tablespoon butter in a skillet. Cool to room temperature and sprinkle with the garlic, salt and pepper. Combine with the wine and enough chicken broth to just cover in a saucepan. Simmer for 15 minutes. Add the carrots and simmer for 15 minutes longer or until the chicken is tender.

Sauté the mushrooms, onion and chiles in 1 tablespoon olive oil and 1 tablespoon butter in a skillet. Add to the the chicken mixture and remove from the heat. Let stand until cool. Chill in the refrigerator for 2 to 12 hours.

Skim the surface of the cooking liquid and reheat the chicken mixture. Remove 1/4 cup of the cooking liquid and blend it into the flour in a small bowl. Add to the saucepan and cook until slightly thickened, stirring constantly. Serve with crusty French bread.

NOTE: DISCARD THE SEEDS AND MEMBRANES OF THE CHILES FOR A MILDER TASTE.

*Serves four*

# COUNTRY HERB-BAKED CHICKEN

| | |
|---|---|
| $^{1}/_{2}$ | cup low-fat yogurt |
| 2 | teaspoons Dijon mustard |
| $^{1}/_{4}$ | teaspoon salt |
| $^{1}/_{8}$ | teaspoon pepper |
| 4 | boneless skinless chicken breasts |
| 1 | cup bread crumbs |
| 3 | tablespoons chopped fresh parsley |
| 2 | tablespoons grated Parmesan cheese |
| 1 | teaspoon paprika |
| 1 | teaspoon dried basil |
| $^{1}/_{2}$ | teaspoon dried tarragon |
| $^{1}/_{2}$ | teaspoon dried thyme |
| 2 | tablespoons butter, melted |

Combine the yogurt, Dijon mustard, salt and pepper in a medium bowl and mix well. Add the chicken, turning to coat well. Marinate, covered with plastic wrap, in the refrigerator for 15 minutes.

Mix the bread crumbs, parsley, cheese, paprika, basil, tarragon and thyme in a shallow dish. Add the melted butter and toss to mix well.

Line a baking sheet with foil and spray with nonstick cooking spray. Remove the chicken from the marinade and coat with the bread crumb mixture, pressing to coat well. Arrange on the prepared baking sheet. Bake at 375 degrees for 35 minutes.

*Serves four*

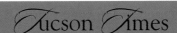

### NATIVE AMERICANS

The Tucson area is home to two major Native American reservations. The Tohono O'odham nation has 2.8 million acres and nearly 19,000 members. The Pascua Yaqui nation has 895 acres and 9,000 members. Gaming casinos operate on both reservations.

# GRILLED LEMON CINNAMON CHICKEN

1/2 cup fresh lemon juice
1/2 teaspoon tomato paste
1 teaspoon minced jalapeño chile
3 garlic cloves, minced
1/2 tablespoon ground cinnamon
1 tablespoon chopped fresh oregano, or 1 teaspoon dried oregano
Salt and freshly ground pepper to taste
4 boneless skinless chicken breasts

Mix the lemon juice, tomato paste, chile, garlic, cinnamon and oregano in a bowl. Season with salt and pepper. Add the chicken, turning to coat well. Marinate, covered with plastic wrap, in the refrigerator for 2 to 8 hours, turning occasionally.

Drain the chicken, discarding the marinade. Place on an oiled rack over hot coals and grill for 5 to 6 minutes on each side or until cooked through.

NOTE: NUTRITIONAL ANALYSIS INCLUDES THE ENTIRE AMOUNT OF THE MARINADE.

Serves four

# HONEY-BAKED CHICKEN

4 boneless skinless chicken breasts
1/4 cup honey
1 tablespoon reduced-sodium soy sauce
2 tablespoons chicken broth
1/2 teaspoon chili powder

Arrange the chicken in an 8 × 8-inch baking dish sprayed with nonstick cooking spray.

Combine the honey, soy sauce, chicken broth and chili powder in a bowl and mix well. Spoon over the chicken. Bake at 325 degrees for 45 minutes or until cooked through, basting occasionally.

NOTE: INCREASE THE OVEN TEMPERATURE TO 350 DEGREES FOR A METAL PAN.

Serves four

# GRILLED MEDITERRANEAN CHICKEN WITH FENNEL SEEDS

1   cup packed coarsely
    chopped cilantro
4   scallions with tops,
    thinly sliced
4   garlic cloves, chopped
2   tablespoons fennel
    seeds, toasted, crushed
1   tablespoon grated
    gingerroot
1   tablespoon hot
    Hungarian paprika
1   teaspoon ground cumin
1/4 teaspoon saffron
    threads, finely chopped
1/2 teaspoon salt
1   teaspoon cayenne
    pepper
1   tablespoon olive oil
1/4 cup fresh lemon juice
1/2 cup water
6   boneless skinless
    chicken breasts,
    trimmed

Combine the cilantro, scallions, garlic, fennel seeds, gingerroot, paprika, cumin, saffron, salt and cayenne pepper in a large nonreactive bowl. Add the olive oil, lemon juice and water and mix well. Add the chicken and toss to coat well. Marinate, covered, in the refrigerator for 8 hours or longer.

Drain the chicken, discarding the marinade. Place on a rack sprayed with nonstick cooking spray over hot coals. Grill for 4 to 5 minutes on each side or until the juices run clear.

*Serves six*

## Cooking Tips

### TOASTING SEEDS

Toasting fennel seeds, pine nuts, and other seeds intensifies their flavor. Sprinkle the seeds in an ungreased skillet and cook over medium-high heat for 2 to 3 minutes or until golden brown, stirring constantly. Seeds may also be toasted in a 350-degree oven until golden brown, stirring occasionally and watching closely to prevent overbrowning.

# CHICKEN BREASTS STUFFED WITH GOAT CHEESE AND BASIL

**Chicken**

4 boneless skinless
  chicken breasts
1/2 cup fresh goat cheese
2 green onions,
  thinly sliced
3 basil leaves, shredded,
  or 1 teaspoon
  dried basil
  Salt and freshly ground
  pepper to taste
1 egg, beaten
1/2 cup dry bread crumbs
2 tablespoons unsalted
  butter, melted

**Mushroom Wine Sauce**

8 ounces mushrooms,
  sliced
1/4 cup (1/2 stick) unsalted
  butter, melted
1/2 cup dry white wine
2/3 cup chicken stock or
  reduced-sodium broth
1/4 cup (1/2 stick) chilled
  unsalted butter, cut
  into tablespoons
  Salt and freshly ground
  pepper to taste

*For the chicken*, pound the chicken with a meat mallet to 1/4-inch thickness between waxed paper; pat dry.

Combine the goat cheese, green onions, basil, salt and pepper in a small bowl and mix well. Spread the mixture lengthwise over half of each piece of chicken. Tuck in the ends and roll the chicken tightly from the long side; secure with string.

Dip the rolls into the egg, allowing the excess to drip into the bowl. Roll in the bread crumbs, shaking off the excess.

Arrange the rolls in an 8 × 8-inch baking dish. Drizzle with the butter. Bake at 350 degrees for 20 minutes or until cooked through.

*For the sauce*, sauté the mushrooms in 1/4 cup melted butter in a large heavy skillet over medium heat for 8 minutes or until tender. Add the wine and cook for 3 minutes. Add the chicken stock and cook for 6 minutes or until the liquid is reduced by half.

Remove from the heat and swirl in 1/4 cup butter 1 tablespoon at a time. Season with salt and pepper.

*To serve*, remove the string from the chicken and cut crosswise into 1/2-inch slices. Fan the slices on serving plates and serve with the sauce.

*Serves four*

# Moroccan Chicken Stew

3 pounds chicken pieces
1 tablespoon vegetable oil
1 large onion, chopped
1 garlic clove, minced
1 tablespoon ground coriander
1¹/2 teaspoons ground cumin
1 teaspoon ground cinnamon
1 teaspoon ground ginger
1 teaspoon ground turmeric
¹/2 teaspoon salt
¹/4 teaspoon red pepper flakes
1 (14-ounce) can tomatoes
³/4 cup water
12 ounces carrots, sliced diagonally
¹/4 cup toasted almonds
1¹/2 teaspoons confectioners' sugar
¹/2 teaspoon ground cinnamon
1 tablespoon minced fresh parsley

Cook half the chicken at a time in the heated oil in a large skillet for 10 minutes or until brown on both sides. Remove to a platter and drain the skillet.

Add the onion and garlic to the skillet and sauté for 5 minutes. Stir in the coriander, cumin, 1 teaspoon cinnamon, ginger, turmeric, salt and red pepper flakes.

Add the undrained tomatoes and water, stirring to break up the tomatoes. Add the chicken and carrots. Bring to a boil and reduce the heat. Simmer, covered, for 35 minutes.

Process the almonds, confectioners' sugar and ¹/2 teaspoon cinnamon in a food processor or blender until the almonds are finely chopped. Serve the stew over hot couscous and sprinkle the servings with the parsley and almond mixture.

*Serves six*

## About Thyme

### DRIED AND FRESH HERBS

Dried herbs are more concentrated than fresh herbs. Use three times the amount of fresh herbs as the dried herbs called for in the recipe. Store dried herbs in an airtight container in a cool dark place to keep them from losing their flavor.

# Orange Marmalade Chicken

Zest of 1 orange
4 chicken breasts
$^1/4$ cup ($^1/2$ stick) butter
$^1/4$ cup Grand Marnier
1 cup chicken bouillon
1 (11-ounce) can
 mandarin oranges
1 tablespoon flour
1 tablespoon lemon juice
2 tablespoons orange
 marmalade

Combine the orange zest with water to cover in a small saucepan and simmer for 10 minutes; drain and reserve the zest.

Sauté the chicken in the butter in a skillet until nearly cooked through. Remove the chicken to a baking dish and drain the excess drippings from the skillet.

Add the Grand Marnier to the skillet and ignite. Allow the flames to die down and add the chicken bouillon, stirring to deglaze the skillet.

Drain the mandarin oranges, reserving the oranges and 3 tablespoons juice. Combine the flour with the reserved orange juice, lemon juice and marmalade in a small bowl and mix well. Add to the skillet with the reserved zest. Cook until thickened, stirring constantly.

Spoon over the chicken. Add the mandarin oranges. Bake at 350 degrees for 20 minutes or until bubbly.

NOTE: YOU MAY ADD $^1/2$ TABLESPOON CORNSTARCH TO THE SAUCE IF NEEDED FOR THE DESIRED CONSISTENCY.

Serves four

# EL CHARRO CAFE

*El Charro is the nation's oldest Mexican restaurant, having been continuously operated by the same family since 1922.*
*Monica Flin opened the cafe, which is housed in the original Flin home built by her father in 1896. Julius Flin*
*constructed his family home with the dark volcanic stone quarried from Sentinel Peak, known as "A" Mountain.*
*Monica was a one-woman show when she opened her cafe in 1922. She was the cook, waitress, cleaner, and hostess.*
*Tucsonans welcomed her authentic Mexican cuisine, and her operations grew ever more successful.*
*Over seventy-five years later, Monica's great-niece Carlotta Flores and her family continue the tradition.*
*El Charro is famous for its carne seca, a flavorful and spicy dried beef dish. Passersby can see strips of beef sun-drying*
*in a cage atop the historic cafe's roof, just as it was done when the restaurant first opened.*

# SICILIAN ROASTED CHICKEN

8    chicken breasts
Olive oil
3 or 4 bay leaves
2 or 3 garlic cloves, chopped
Parsley flakes, oregano, salt
      and pepper to taste
2    large tomatoes, sliced
1    (8-ounce) jar large
     pitted green olives,
     drained
Butter
1    cup (or more) water
2    (8-ounce) cans whole
     mushrooms, drained
3/4  cup sherry

Arrange the chicken in a roasting pan coated with olive oil. Sprinkle with the bay leaves, garlic, parsley flakes, oregano, salt and pepper. Add the tomatoes and olives and sprinkle with salt. Dot with butter and pour the water into the pan.

Roast at 350 degrees for 1 hour. Add the mushrooms, sherry and additional water if needed. Roast for 15 minutes longer; discard the bay leaves. Serve with rice, a salad, the pan juices and garlic bread for dipping.

*Serves eight*

## Tucson Times

### COLOSSAL CAVE

There is evidence that the ocean once covered Colossal Cave, a massive underground labyrinth located twenty miles southeast of downtown Tucson. Discovered in 1879, it is now listed in the National Register of Historic Places. It is one of the largest dry caverns in the world, and has never been explored to its end.

# SMOKED CHICKEN IN MUSTARD SAUCE

**Mustard Sauce**

1 1/2 cups mayonnaise
3/4  cup Dijon mustard
1/4  cup orange juice
1    tablespoon grated
     orange zest
1/2  teaspoon freshly
     grated pepper

**Chicken**

2    ounces liquid smoke
8    boneless skinless
     chicken breasts
1/2  cup (1 stick) butter,
     melted
4    avocados, sliced

*For the sauce,* combine the mayonnaise, Dijon mustard, orange juice, orange zest and pepper in a bowl and mix well. Chill until serving time.

*For the chicken,* combine the liquid smoke with the chicken in a shallow dish and turn to coat well. Marinate, covered, in the refrigerator for 8 hours or longer, turning several times.

Sauté the chicken in the melted butter in a skillet until cooked through. Remove to a platter and let stand until cool. Cut diagonally into slices.

*To serve,* arrange the chicken slices and avocados on a serving platter or serving plates. Serve with the sauce.

*Serves eight*

# Spicy Chicken with Black Bean Purée

**Chicken**

4    teaspoons fajita seasoning

4    boneless skinless chicken breasts

2    teaspoons olive oil

**Black Bean Purée**

1    cup chopped onion

4    garlic cloves, minced

2    (15-ounce) cans black beans

2    small Roma tomatoes, chopped

1/4    cup chopped cilantro

2    tablespoons lime juice

1    teaspoon ground cumin

1/2    teaspoon ground red pepper

*For the chicken*, rub the fajita seasoning over the chicken. Sauté in the heated olive oil in a skillet until cooked through; remove the chicken from the skillet, reserving the drippings.

*For the purée*, add the onion and garlic to the drippings in the skillet. Sauté until tender.

Drain the beans, reserving the liquid. Rinse the beans and drain again. Combine the beans, reserved liquid, tomatoes, cilantro, lime juice, cumin and red pepper in a food processor or blender container. Add the sautéed onion and garlic. Process until smooth.

Pour the purée into a small saucepan. Cook until heated through. Spoon over the chicken.

NOTE: YOU MAY TOP WITH SHREDDED MONTEREY JACK CHEESE IF DESIRED.

*Serves four*

# TEX-MEX CHICKEN AND PEPPERS

1   pound boneless skinless
    chicken breasts
2   tablespoons plus
    1¹/2 teaspoons
    vegetable oil
2   red bell peppers, cut
    into thin strips
1   large garlic clove,
    thinly sliced
1   medium onion, cut into
    thin wedges
1   teaspoon oregano
1   teaspoon salt
1¹/2 cups salsa
1   (15-ounce) can black
    beans, drained, rinsed
2   tablespoons minced
    fresh cilantro

Cut the chicken into thin strips. Sauté in 2 tablespoons of the oil in a medium skillet over high heat for 5 minutes or until cooked through. Remove the chicken to a plate with a slotted spoon.

Add the remaining 1¹/2 teaspoons oil to the skillet and add the bell peppers, garlic, onion, oregano and salt. Sauté for 5 minutes or until tender, stirring frequently.

Return the chicken to the skillet and add the salsa and beans. Cook until heated through. Sprinkle with the cilantro and serve with warm flour tortillas or tortilla chips.

Serves six

---

## Tucson Times

### MOUNTAIN NAMES

Both the Santa Catalina Mountains and Mount Lemmon are named for women. Father Kino named the mountains for his sister Catarina, a name which later evolved into Catalina. Mount Lemmon was named for Sara Lemmon, who climbed the north side of the mountain on horseback while on her honeymoon and kept a diary of her adventures and encounters with a mountain lion, bears, and bobcats.

# THYME CHICKEN IN PASTRY

8 boneless skinless
   chicken breasts
2 teaspoons thyme
Salt and pepper to taste
5 tablespoons butter
1 large onion, finely
   chopped
8 ounces mushrooms,
   sliced
2 tablespoons chopped
   fresh parsley
2 sheets frozen puff
   pastry, thawed
8 ounces cream cheese,
   softened
2 tablespoons Dijon
   mustard
1 egg, beaten
2 teaspoons water

Sprinkle the chicken with the thyme, salt and pepper. Brown on both sides in 3 tablespoons of the butter in a skillet; remove with a slotted spoon. Add the remaining 2 tablespoons butter to the skillet. Add the onion and mushrooms and sauté until the onion is tender and the liquid from the mushrooms has evaporated. Stir in the parsley.

Cut each pastry sheet into 4 squares on a lightly floured surface. Roll each into a 7-inch square.

Combine the cream cheese and mustard in a small bowl and mix well. Spoon into the center of each pastry square. Top with the mushroom mixture and a chicken breast. Brush the edges of the pastry with water and wrap to enclose the filling completely; press the edges to seal.

Place seam side down on an ungreased baking sheet. Brush with a mixture of the egg and 2 teaspoons water. Bake at 375 degrees for 25 minutes or until puffed and golden brown.

*Serves eight*

## About Thyme

### AN UNUSUAL THYME

Some of the more unusual kinds of thyme are Silver Posie, Variegated, and Doone Valley. Silver Posie is a shrub with pale pink or lilac flowers and leaves edged in silver. Variegated Thyme can be substituted for ordinary thyme, but is harder for the gardener to grow. Doone Valley Thyme has pale purple flowers which attract bees; the honey made from this variety is highly prized.

# GRILLED CORNISH GAME HENS
## MONT VENTOUX

1/3 cup coarse or
kosher salt
10 garlic cloves
6 (13-ounce) Cornish
game hens, or
12 chicken breasts
1/4 cup olive oil
1/4 cup minced fresh
thyme, mint, marjoram
or basil
1/4 teaspoon salt
1/4 teaspoon pepper
6 thin (5-inch) zucchini
6 leeks, white portion
only
3 Japanese eggplant, cut
into halves
2 red bell peppers, cut
into quarters, seeded
1 1/2 cups crumbled
feta cheese
1/4 cup minced fresh
thyme, mint, marjoram
or basil

Combine the coarse salt and garlic with enough water to measure 4 cups in a blender container and process until the garlic is puréed. Pour over the game hens in a large nonreactive bowl. Marinate, covered, in the refrigerator for 8 to 24 hours.

Combine the olive oil, 1/4 cup fresh herbs, 1/4 teaspoon salt and pepper in a large bowl. Add the zucchini, leeks, eggplant and bell peppers and mix well. Let stand at room temperature for 1 hour.

Arrange the leeks around the outer edge of a rack over hot coals. Grill for 10 minutes. Arrange the remaining vegetables around the outer edge of the rack and grill for 10 minutes.

Drain the game hens. Place in the center of the rack. Grill for 25 minutes or until the hen legs move easily and the vegetables are tender-crisp.

Remove the hens and vegetables to an oven-proof platter and sprinkle with the cheese. Broil just until the cheese melts. Sprinkle with 1/4 cup fresh herbs. Serve with Spaghetti Vinaigrette (page 61).

*Serves six*

# QUAIL WITH RED CURRANT SAUCE

## Quail
48 slices bacon
24 wild quail, dressed
Flour
1 bunch celery, chopped
3 onions, coarsely
chopped
10 carrots, sliced
1 gallon chicken stock
2 teaspoons thyme
1 tablespoon kosher salt
1 teaspoon freshly ground
pepper

## Red Currant Sauce
1 (8-ounce) jar wild
currant jelly
Juice of 2 lemons
Grated zest of 2 lemons

*For the quail,* fry the bacon in a heavy skillet until nearly crisp; remove the bacon, reserving the drippings in the skillet. Coat the quail with flour and add to the skillet. Cook until brown on all sides.

Sprinkle the celery, onions and carrots in a Dutch oven and arrange the quail on the top. Arrange the bacon over the quail. Add the chicken stock and sprinkle with the thyme, salt and pepper. Bring to a simmer on the stove top and place in a 350-degree oven. Bake for 35 minutes.

*For the sauce,* combine the jelly, lemon juice and lemon zest in a small saucepan. Simmer for 3 to 4 minutes. Cool slightly.

*To serve,* remove the quail from the Dutch oven and drain. Arrange on a platter and serve with the sauce.

*Serves twelve*

## Cooking Tips

### COOKING BACON
To avoid spattering and to keep bacon from curling, bake it in the oven. Place the slices on a foil-lined baking sheet for easier cleanup and bake at 350 degrees for 6 minutes. Turn the bacon and bake for 2 to 3 minutes longer or until as crisp as desired.

# Turkey Pie with Black Beans and Corn

## Cheese Pastry

2 cups flour
1/2 cup finely shredded Cheddar cheese
2/3 cup plain or butter-flavor shortening
5 to 6 tablespoons cold water

## Filling

1 (8-ounce) potato, cut into 1/2-inch slices
1 medium onion, chopped
1 tablespoon vegetable oil
3 cups coarsely chopped cooked turkey
1 (16-ounce) can black beans, drained
1 (14-ounce) can Mexican-style stewed tomatoes
1 (16-ounce) can whole kernel corn, drained
1 (4-ounce) jar sliced pimentos, drained
1 teaspoon chili powder
1 1/2 cups shredded Cheddar cheese

*For the pastry,* toss the flour and cheese in a medium bowl. Cut in the shortening with a pastry blender or 2 knives until the mixture resembles coarse crumbs. Add the water 1 tablespoon at a time, mixing with a fork after each addition until the mixture is moist enough to form a dough. Shape into a ball and cover with plastic wrap.

*For the filling,* combine the potato with water to cover in a saucepan and bring to a boil over high heat. Reduce the heat and simmer, covered, for 5 minutes or until the potato is tender; drain.

Sauté the onion in the heated oil in a 12-inch skillet until tender, stirring occasionally. Stir in the turkey, beans, tomatoes, corn, pimentos, potato and chili powder. Bring to a boil over high heat and remove from the heat. Stir in the cheese.

*To assemble,* divide the dough into 1/3 and 2/3 portions. Roll the larger portion into a 14-inch circle on a lightly floured surface. Fit gently into a 9-inch pie plate. Trim the edge, leaving a 1-inch overhang.

Spoon the turkey mixture into the prepared pie plate. Roll the remaining dough into an 11-inch circle on a floured surface. Place over the turkey mixture and trim, leaving a 1-inch overhang. Fold under the overhanging pastry and flute the edge; cut vents in the top.

Bake at 400 degrees for 40 to 45 minutes or until the filling is bubbly and the crust is golden brown.

*Serves six to eight*

# Temptations from the Waters

SEAFOOD

# FINE ARTS EVENING

*Friends often gather for a savory dinner before heading
out to a show. Tucson offers many fine arts events to enjoy, from
exhibits at the Tucson Museum of Art to performances with
the Tucson Symphony Orchestra, the Arizona Opera Company,
or the Arizona Theatre Company, to name just
a few. Food and art have always been a good combination.*

## Menu

CHEESY RYE TOASTS

HEARTS OF PALM AND ALMOND SALAD

PAN-SEARED SCALLOPS
WITH GINGER ORANGE SPINACH

LEMON BASIL POTATO PUFF

BROWN SUGAR-GLAZED CARROTS

DILL POPOVERS

CHOCOLATE MOUSSE TERRINE

COFFEE AND TEA

# SOUTHWEST BARBECUED HALIBUT WITH PAPAYA SALSA

**Chimichurri**

3   bunches green onions,
    chopped
1 1/2 teaspoons salt
1/4  teaspoon crushed red
    pepper flakes
Lemon juice
Olive oil

**Papaya Salsa**

1   (26-ounce) jar papaya,
    drained, chopped
2   tablespoons lime juice
1   tablespoon brown sugar
1   small onion, chopped
1   red bell pepper, chopped
1/4  teaspoon crushed red
    pepper flakes
2   tablespoons minced
    fresh basil

**Halibut**

4   halibut fillets
1   cup chimichurri
3   (16-ounce) cans refried
    black beans
Chicken broth
1/2  head lettuce, chopped

*For the chimichurri,* combine the green onions, salt and red pepper flakes in a 1-pint jar. Add enough lemon juice to measure 1/4 of the way up the side of the jar. Fill the remainder of the jar with olive oil. Store in the refrigerator.

*For the salsa,* combine the papaya, lime juice, brown sugar, onion, bell pepper, and red pepper flakes in a bowl and mix well. Chill until serving time. Add the basil just before serving.

*To prepare the dish,* combine the halibut with 1 cup of the chimichurri in a shallow dish. Marinate in the refrigerator for 1 to 3 hours. Drain, reserving the marinade. Grill the halibut over hot coals just until opaque, basting frequently with the reserved marinade. Bring any remaining marinade to a boil in a small saucepan.

Heat the beans in a saucepan, adding a small amount of chicken broth if necessary for the desired consistency. Mound in the center of a serving platter and top with the lettuce. Arrange the halibut over the lettuce and spoon the heated marinade over the top. Serve with the salsa.

*Serves four*

# TACOS DE PESCADO

## Chile Salsa

| | |
|---|---|
| 1/4 | cup chopped cilantro |
| 3 | green onions |
| 2 | tomatoes, cut into quarters |
| 1 | jalapeño chile |
| 3 | serrano chiles |
| 1 | yellow bell pepper, cut into quarters |
| 2 | tomatillos |
| 2 | tablespoons light mayonnaise |

## Tacos

| | |
|---|---|
| 1 | pound halibut or shark |
| 1 | tablespoon olive oil |
| 1 | garlic clove, chopped |
| | Ground oregano and ground cumin to taste |
| | Salt and pepper to taste |
| 6 | corn tortillas |
| | Juice of 1 lime |
| 3 | cups finely shredded cabbage |
| 1 | cup shredded Monterey Jack cheese |

*For the salsa*, combine the cilantro, green onions, tomatoes, chiles, bell pepper and tomatillos in a food processor container and process until coarsely chopped. Combine with the mayonnaise in a bowl and mix well.

*For the tacos*, brush the halibut with the olive oil and sprinkle with garlic, oregano, cumin, salt and pepper. Place on a sheet of foil on the grill rack. Grill until cooked through.

Cut the halibut into 6 pieces and place each on a tortilla. Top with the salsa, lime juice, cabbage and cheese. Serve with refried beans and strawberry margaritas.

*Serves six*

# CITRUS RED SNAPPER

6   (4-ounce) red snapper
     or other lean white
     fish fillets
1   carrot, julienned
1   green onion, julienned
3   tablespoons thawed
     frozen orange juice
     concentrate
$^1/_4$   cup water
1   tablespoon olive oil
1   teaspoon grated
     orange zest
$^1/_4$   teaspoon ground
     nutmeg
$^1/_2$   teaspoon coarsely
     ground pepper
12   thin orange wedges
6   cilantro sprigs

Arrange the red snapper in an 8 × 12-inch baking dish sprayed with nonstick cooking spray. Sprinkle with the carrot and green onion.

Combine the orange juice concentrate, water, olive oil, orange zest, nutmeg and pepper in a bowl and mix well. Pour over the red snapper and vegetables.

Bake at 350 degrees for 20 to 25 minutes or just until the fillets flake easily. Top with the orange wedges and cilantro.

Serves six

# BASIL AND GARLIC SALMON FILLET

1/2   cup (1 stick) butter
1/2   (10-ounce) bottle white
      wine Worcestershire
      sauce
1/8   teaspoon chopped garlic
1/8   teaspoon celery salt
1/4   teaspoon dried
      sweet basil
1/8   teaspoon white pepper
1     (2-pound) salmon fillet

Combine the butter, Worcestershire sauce, garlic, celery salt, basil and white pepper in a saucepan. Bring to a boil and reduce the heat. Simmer for 10 minutes.

Place the salmon in a baking dish with a cover. Pour the butter mixture over the salmon. Bake, covered, at 350 degrees for 10 minutes or until the fillet flakes easily.

NOTE: IF MORE LIQUID IS NEEDED, ADD WHITE WINE.

*Serves four*

## Beverage Tips

### QUICK FROZEN MARGARITAS

Combine one 6-ounce can frozen limeade concentrate, 1/2 cup orange juice, 3/4 cup tequila, and ice cubes in a blender container and process until smooth. Serve with lime wedges.

# GRILLED SALMON WITH SPICE CRUST AND CORN SALSA

**Salmon**

1¹/2 tablespoons coriander seeds
1¹/2 tablespoons mustard seeds
1¹/2 tablespoons cumin seeds
1    teaspoon black peppercorns
3    tablespoons light brown sugar
1    (4-pound) boneless salmon fillet with skin

**Corn Salsa**

6    cups fresh or frozen corn kernels
Salt to taste
2    tablespoons reserved spice mixture
1    cup finely chopped red onion
¹/2  cup olive oil
¹/4  cup lime juice
¹/2  cup chopped fresh cilantro
1¹/2 tablespoons minced seeded jalapeño chile

*For the salmon*, heat a small heavy skillet over high heat. Add the coriander seeds, mustard seeds and cumin seeds and toast for 3 minutes or until fragrant. Combine with the peppercorns and grind until fine. Mix with the brown sugar in a bowl. Reserve 2 tablespoons of the mixture for the salsa.

Rub the remaining spice mixture over the salmon, pressing gently to coat well. Place on a plate, cover with plastic wrap and chill for 1 to 12 hours.

*For the salsa*, cook the corn in salted water to cover in a saucepan for 2 minutes; drain. Combine with the reserved spice mixture, onion, olive oil, lime juice, cilantro and chile in a bowl and mix well. Season with salt. Chill, covered, for 1 to 4 hours.

*To cook the salmon*, grill skin side down on a rack over medium coals for 6 minutes on each side or until opaque. Serve with the salsa.

*Serves twelve*

# WINE-POACHED SALMON

1/2  cup white wine
8  cups (or more) water
2  bay leaves
10  peppercorns
1  lemon, cut into halves
1  (3-pound) salmon fillet

Combine the wine, water, bay leaves and peppercorns in a large shallow pan. Squeeze in the juice of the lemon and add the squeezed lemon halves to the pan. Bring to a boil and reduce the heat.

Trim the skin from the salmon and cut into 3/4-inch slices. Place in the simmering liquid; the liquid should cover the salmon completely. Poach, uncovered, for 3 to 5 minutes or until the fillet flakes easily; do not overcook.

Remove to a platter with a slotted spoon to cool completely. Layer the slices in a shallow dish with waxed paper between the layers. Chill, covered with plastic wrap, in the refrigerator for up to 12 hours. Serve cold with Mustard Dill Sauce (page 50).

*Serves twelve*

## Cooking Tips

### COOKING FRESH FISH

It is easy to determine the length of time to cook fresh fish. Place the fish on its side and measure it at its thickest section. Cook it for 10 minutes for each inch, regardless of method. To prevent it from curling during cooking, place it skin side down in the skillet first.

# DILLED DIJON SEA BASS

1 cup country-style
   Dijon mustard
1/2 cup chardonnay
5 to 6 garlic cloves, minced
1/4 cup drained capers
4 (5-ounce) sea bass
   fillets
8 fresh dill sprigs

Combine the Dijon mustard, wine, garlic and capers in a dish and mix well. Add the sea bass, turning to coat well. Arrange the sea bass in a shallow baking dish, placing 1 sprig of fresh dill under and 1 sprig of fresh dill on top of each fillet.

Pour the wine mixture over the fillets. Marinate, covered with plastic wrap, in the refrigerator for 1 to 3 hours. Bake at 350 degrees until the fillets flake easily.

NOTE: YOU MAY ALSO REMOVE THE FISH FROM THE MARINADE AND GRILL UNTIL IT FLAKES EASILY, BASTING WITH THE MARINADE. BRING ANY REMAINING MARINADE TO A BOIL IN A SAUCEPAN TO SERVE IT WITH THE FISH. NUTRITIONAL ANALYSIS INCLUDES THE ENTIRE AMOUNT OF THE MARINADE.

Serves four

## Cooking Tips

### THAWING FISH

Do not thaw frozen fish at room temperature or in warm water, as this causes the fish to lose moisture and flavor. Thaw the fish in the refrigerator, allowing 18 to 24 hours of thawing time per pound. For the best results, cook fish immediately after thawing and never refreeze fish that has been thawed.

# SAKE-MARINATED SEA BASS WITH
# COCONUT CURRY SAUCE

### Sake Marinade and Sea Bass

| | |
|---|---|
| 1/4 | cup sake |
| 1/2 | cup mirin |
| 1/4 | cup tamari or soy sauce |
| 2 | tablespoons yellow miso |
| 2 | tablespoons rice vinegar |
| 1 | tablespoon chopped gingerroot |
| 1 | tablespoon brown sugar |
| 6 | (6-ounce) sea bass fillets |
| 1 | tablespoon vegetable oil |

### Coconut Curry Sauce

| | |
|---|---|
| 1/2 | cup mirin |
| 1/4 | cup chopped fresh lemon grass |
| 1 | tablespoon chopped gingerroot |
| 1/4 | cup dry chardonnay |
| 2 | cups heavy cream |
| 3/4 | cup canned unsweetened coconut milk |
| 2 | tablespoons Thai red curry paste |

Salt and pepper to taste

*For the marinade,* combine the sake, mirin, tamari, miso, vinegar, gingerroot and brown sugar in a blender container and process until smooth.

*To marinate the sea bass,* arrange the fillets in a single layer in a shallow dish. Pour the marinade over the fillets. Marinate, covered, in the refrigerator for 2 hours, turning occasionally.

*To cook the sea bass,* remove the fillets from the marinade. Sear on both sides in the heated oil in a nonstick ovenproof skillet over medium-high heat for 2 minutes or until golden brown. Bake at 400 degrees for 10 to 15 minutes or until the fillets flake easily; keep warm.

*For the sauce,* combine the mirin, lemon grass and gingerroot in a small saucepan and boil for 6 minutes or until reduced to 1/4 cup. Add the wine and boil for 6 minutes or until reduced again to 1/4 cup.

Stir in the cream and coconut milk. Bring to a boil and reduce the heat. Simmer for 12 minutes or until slightly thickened, stirring occasionally. Stir in the curry paste, salt and pepper.

Serve the fillets over beds of hot steamed rice and spoon the sauce over the top.

*Serves six*

# SWORDFISH WITH GINGER AND LEMON

Juice and grated zest of
  2 lemons
2  tablespoons
   vegetable oil
1  tablespoon soy sauce
2  tablespoons minced
   gingerroot
2  scallions, thinly sliced
1/2  teaspoon salt
1/8  teaspoon cayenne
   pepper
4  (6-ounce) swordfish
   steaks, 1 inch thick

Combine the lemon juice, lemon zest, oil, soy sauce, gingerroot, scallions, salt and cayenne pepper in a shallow dish and mix well. Add the swordfish, turning to coat well. Marinate at room temperature for 45 minutes, turning occasionally.

Remove the swordfish from the marinade and place on a rack in a broiler pan. Broil for 3 to 4 minutes on each side or until the steaks flake easily.

NOTE: NUTRITIONAL ANALYSIS INCLUDES THE ENTIRE AMOUNT OF THE MARINADE.

Serves four

## Cooking Tips

### JUICING LEMONS

To get more juice from lemons, store them in a tightly sealed jar of water in the refrigerator. They will also yield more juice if they are rolled on a hard surface before cutting. This is true for oranges and grapefruit as well.

# LEMON AND BASIL WHITEFISH

1/4 cup chicken broth
3 tablespoons
  orange juice
2 tablespoons lemon juice
1 tablespoon shredded
  lemon zest
2 tablespoons olive oil
4 (6-ounce) whitefish
  fillets
8 whole fresh basil leaves

Combine the chicken broth, orange juice, lemon juice, lemon zest and olive oil in a 10- to 12-inch skillet. Cover and bring to a boil. Add the fillets in a single layer. Reduce the heat.

Simmer, covered, for 4 minutes. Place basil leaves on top of the fillets. Simmer just until the fillets flake easily but are still moist. Remove the whitefish to a serving platter.

Boil the cooking liquid, uncovered, for 2 to 3 minutes or until reduced to 1/4 cup. Spoon over the whitefish.

*Serves four*

# CRISPY BAY SCALLOPS

5 slices white bread,
  trimmed
1 1/2 pounds scallops
Salt and pepper to taste
1/4 cup (1/2 stick) butter,
  melted
1/4 cup fresh basil,
  shredded
Juice of 1 lime

Process the bread in a food processor until finely crumbled. Place in a shallow dish. Sprinkle the scallops with salt and pepper. Dredge in the bread crumbs. Arrange on a baking sheet. Drizzle with the butter.

Broil 4 to 5 inches from the heat source for 7 minutes or until golden brown. Arrange the scallops on a serving platter. Sprinkle with the basil, lime juice, salt and pepper.

*Serve six to eight*

# Pan-Seared Scallops with Ginger Orange Spinach

1 tablespoon julienned gingerroot
1 tablespoon sliced green onions
4 garlic cloves, chopped
1/2 cup vodka
1/4 cup dry vermouth
20 sea scallops, about 1 1/2 pounds
1/2 cup (1 stick) butter
1 teaspoon grated orange zest
1/3 cup fresh orange juice
1 1/2 pounds fresh spinach, chopped
1/2 teaspoon salt
1/8 teaspoon pepper

Combine the gingerroot, green onions and garlic in a small bowl and mix well. Combine half the mixture with the vodka and vermouth in a shallow dish and mix well. Add the scallops and toss to coat well. Marinate, covered, in the refrigerator for 30 minutes.

Melt the butter in a large skillet over high heat. Add the remaining ginger mixture and sauté for 30 seconds. Add the orange zest and orange juice and bring to a boil. Stir in the spinach, salt and pepper. Sauté for 2 minutes or until the spinach wilts. Remove to a serving plate with a slotted spoon and keep warm.

Drain the scallops, reserving the marinade. Spray a skillet with nonstick cooking spray and heat over high heat. Add the scallops and cook for 1 1/2 minutes on each side or until golden brown. Arrange over the spinach.

Add the reserved marinade to the skillet, stirring to deglaze. Cook for 5 minutes or until reduced to 1/4 cup. Drizzle over the scallops and spinach.

*Serves four*

# SABINO CANYON

Sabino Canyon is nestled in the rugged Santa Catalina Mountains. The canyon is one of the most accessible and beautiful desert escapes to explore. Oaks, sycamores, and cottonwoods line the creek's streambed. The lush trees in the canyon attract more than two hundred species of birds, making the area an exceptional place for bird watching. Here visitors can enjoy a riparian habitat rarely seen in the desert.

The canyon has a long history of use that precedes present-day Tucsonans. The Hohokam took advantage of the water in the canyon, constructing irrigation canals for their farming. Centuries later, Apaches also made use of the canyon's water, cool shade, and resources for hunting and gathering. In the 1860s, cavalry soldiers cooled off in the swimming pools while families from Tucson lunched under the trees.

# CRAB AND PASTA CAKES

8   ounces fresh lump crab
     meat, flaked
1   cup cooked spaghetti
     or linguini
2   eggs, beaten
1/4   cup fine dry
     bread crumbs
2   serrano chiles, finely
     chopped, or
     2 tablespoons chopped
     green bell pepper
3   green onions, finely
     chopped
2   tablespoons chopped
     fresh cilantro
2   teaspoons olive oil or
     vegetable oil
1/4   teaspoon salt
1/4   teaspoon pepper
2   tablespoons
     vegetable oil

Pick over the crab meat, discarding any bits of shell. Cut the spaghetti into 1-inch pieces.

Combine the eggs, bread crumbs, chiles, green onions, cilantro, olive oil, salt and pepper in a large bowl. Add the crab meat and spaghetti and mix well. Shape into 12 crab cakes 1/2 inch thick.

Heat the vegetable oil in a large heavy skillet. Add the crab cakes a few at a time and cook for 3 minutes on each side or until golden brown, adding additional vegetable oil if necessary; drain.

Garnish with lime or lemon wedges and serve with Cilantro Lime Mayonnaise (page 54).

*Serves six*

# SHRIMP CREOLE

1/2  onion, chopped
1/2  green bell pepper,
     chopped
2    mushrooms, chopped
2    ribs celery, chopped
2 or 3 garlic cloves, crushed
1    tablespoon olive oil or
     seasoned vegetable oil
1    (16-ounce) can
     seasoned tomato sauce
1    (8-ounce) can seasoned
     tomato sauce
3    bay leaves
2    teaspoons oregano
2    teaspoons Cajun
     seasoning
1    teaspoon sugar, or
     to taste
Salt and pepper to taste
1    pound deveined
     peeled shrimp
2    cups hot cooked rice

Sauté the onion, bell pepper, mushrooms, celery and garlic in the olive oil in a saucepan until tender. Add the tomato sauce, bay leaves, oregano, Cajun seasoning, sugar, salt and pepper. Simmer for 20 minutes.

Add the shrimp. Cook for 8 minutes or until the shrimp are cooked through; do not overcook. Discard the bay leaves and serve over the rice.

NOTE: YOU MAY USE FROZEN SHRIMP, BUT REDUCE THE COOKING TIME TO 5 MINUTES AFTER THE SHRIMP IS ADDED.

*Serves four*

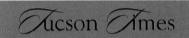

### DESERT VEGETATION

The vegetation of the desert is surprisingly lush. There are several types of trees that thrive in the climate of the high elevation. The Palo Verde, the cottonwood, and the mesquite trees are the most recognizable of the desert trees.

# ONIONY SAUTÉED SHRIMP

White and light green
    portions of 2 leeks,
    thinly sliced
1   cup thinly sliced
    white onion
3   garlic cloves, minced
3   tablespoons
    unsalted butter
$1^1/4$ pounds large shrimp,
    peeled, deveined
2   teaspoons fresh
    lemon juice
2   tablespoons white
    vermouth
Salt and freshly ground
    pepper
2   tablespoons chopped
    fresh parsley

Sauté the leeks, onion and garlic in the butter in a large skillet over low heat for 5 to 6 minutes, stirring occasionally. Remove to a bowl with a slotted spoon. Increase the heat to medium-high.

Add the shrimp and lemon juice to the skillet. Sauté for 1 minute or just until the shrimp begin to turn opaque. Add the vermouth and bring to a boil.

Return the onion mixture to the skillet; season with salt and pepper. Cook until the shrimp are cooked through. Stir in the parsley and serve over rice.

Serves four

## Cooking Tips

### BUYING SEAFOOD FOR TWO

There are some easy guidelines for buying seafood for two. Buy $1^1/3$ pounds whole fish or $1/2$ to $2/3$ pound of fish fillets and $1/2$ to 1 pound shucked or peeled crab meat, lobster, oysters, or shrimp.

# SHRIMP L'AIGLON

2 tablespoons butter
2 shallots, grated
2 garlic cloves, grated
8 ounces (or more) peeled shrimp
2 tablespoons chopped parsley
1 tablespoon chopped chives
1/2 cup bread crumbs

Melt the butter in an ovenproof skillet. Add the shallots, garlic and shrimp. Sauté for 5 to 10 minutes or until the shrimp are cooked through. Stir in the parsley and chives.

Top with the bread crumbs. Broil just until the top is golden brown. Serve over rice or pasta.

*Serves two*

# SHRIMP SCAMPI

2 pounds medium fresh shrimp, peeled, deveined
1/2 cup olive oil
1/2 cup (1 stick) butter
1/2 cup white wine
1/4 cup lemon juice
3 garlic cloves, finely chopped
3 tablespoons chopped parsley
1 teaspoon oregano
Salt and pepper to taste

Arrange the shrimp in a 9 × 13-inch baking dish. Combine the olive oil, butter, wine, lemon juice, garlic, parsley, oregano, salt and pepper in a saucepan. Heat until butter has melted, stirring frequently. Pour over the shrimp. Bake at 375 degrees for 20 minutes or until the shrimp turn pink. Serve with French bread or over rice.

*Serves four to six*

# SHRIMP WITH TOMATOES AND ARUGULA

1³/4 pounds large shrimp in the shell
2 tomatoes, peeled, seeded, chopped
3 scallions, thinly sliced
2 garlic cloves, minced
6 basil leaves, torn
1 bunch arugula or spinach, torn
2¹/2 tablespoons olive oil
1 tablespoon white wine vinegar
¹/4 teaspoon hot pepper sauce
Salt and pepper to taste

Steam the shrimp for 5 minutes or just until cooked through. Cool to room temperature.

Combine the tomatoes, scallions, garlic, basil and arugula in a bowl. Whisk the olive oil, vinegar, pepper sauce, salt and pepper together in a small bowl. Add to the vegetables and toss to coat well.

Peel and devein the shrimp and mound on a serving plate. Spoon the vegetable mixture over the shrimp.

*Serves six*

---

## Cooking Tips

### PEELING AND SEEDING TOMATOES

To peel and seed tomatoes, immerse them in boiling water for about 20 seconds. Remove with a slotted spoon and plunge immediately into ice water. Core the tomatoes with a paring knife and slip off the skins. Cut off and reserve both ends of the tomatoes. Push the seeds out of the center sections with the thumbs and then remove the seeds from the end pieces.

# SEAFOOD IN A LINGUINI SHELL

8    ounces linguini, cooked
1    egg
1/2  cup low-fat ricotta
     cheese
2    tablespoons chopped
     Italian parsley
Freshly ground pepper
     to taste
2 to 6 garlic cloves, chopped
2    tablespoons extra-virgin
     olive oil
1    tablespoon butter
1    onion, chopped
1    cup chopped mixed red,
     green and yellow
     bell peppers
1/2  cup sliced mushrooms
1    pound shrimp, scallops
     and/or crab meat
1 or 2 plum tomatoes,
     chopped
2    tablespoons chopped
     fresh basil
2    teaspoons cornstarch
1/4  cup water
1/2  cup tomato sauce
1/4  cup grated Parmesan
     cheese
1/4  cup shredded
     mozzarella cheese

Combine the cooled pasta with the egg, ricotta cheese, parsley and pepper in a bowl and mix well. Spoon into a greased pie plate and press to form a shell. Bake at 350 degrees for 10 minutes.

Sauté the garlic in the heated olive oil and butter in a skillet over high heat for 1 or 2 minutes. Reduce the heat to medium and add the onion, bell peppers and mushrooms. Sauté until tender.

Add the seafood, tomatoes and basil. Cook until the seafood is cooked through. Blend the cornstarch and water in a small bowl. Add to the seafood mixture and cook until thickened, stirring constantly. Stir in the tomato sauce. Cook until heated through.

Spoon the seafood mixture into the pasta shell. Top with the Parmesan and mozzarella cheeses. Bake for 5 to 10 minutes or until bubbly. Let stand for 5 to 10 minutes before serving.

*Serves four to six*

# Temptations al Dente

## PASTA

# STREET FAIR FINALE

*A favorite event in Tucson enjoyed by young and old alike is the 4th Avenue Street Fair. Artisans line the street selling their creations, while bands play, and delicious food is served. This light menu is the perfect finale to a day of walking and shopping.*

## Menu

ROASTED TOMATO AND
EGGPLANT CROSTINI

SESAME CHICKEN WITH
CRISPY ANGEL HAIR PASTA

ENDIVE AND JICAMA TOSS

CITRUS TIRAMISU

# Mediterranean Spaghetti

8   ounces lean
    ground beef
2   cups chopped onions
2   garlic cloves, minced
1 1/2 teaspoons dried oregano
1/2  cup dry red wine
1/4  cup water
1   (14-ounce) can stewed
    tomatoes
3/4  teaspoon ground
    cinnamon
1/8  teaspoon ground
    nutmeg
1/2  teaspoon salt
1/8  teaspoon pepper
1/4  cup flour
1/4  teaspoon ground
    nutmeg
2   cups 1% milk
1   cup crumbled feta
    cheese
1   tablespoon grated
    Parmesan cheese
1   large egg
2   tablespoons dry
    bread crumbs
8   ounces spaghetti,
    cooked, drained
1   tablespoon grated
    Parmesan cheese

Heat a large nonstick skillet over medium-high heat.
Add the ground beef, onions, garlic and oregano. Cook for
5 minutes, stirring until the ground beef is crumbly; drain.
Add the wine, water, tomatoes, cinnamon, 1/8 teaspoon
nutmeg, salt and pepper. Bring to a boil and reduce the
heat. Simmer for 10 minutes or until thickened.

Blend the flour and 1/4 teaspoon nutmeg with the milk in
a saucepan. Bring to a boil, stirring constantly. Reduce the
heat and simmer for 7 minutes or until thickened, stirring
constantly. Remove from the heat. Stir in the feta cheese
and 1 tablespoon Parmesan cheese until melted. Add the
egg and mix well.

Sprinkle half the bread crumbs in a 2-quart baking dish.
Layer the spaghetti, ground beef mixture and cheese sauce
1/2 at a time in the prepared dish. Top with a mixture
of 1 tablespoon Parmesan cheese and the remaining
1 tablespoon bread crumbs. Bake at 375 degrees for
30 minutes or until golden brown. Let stand for 5 minutes
before serving. Garnish with fresh oregano.

*Serves six*

# YAKASOBA

2 pounds boneless pork, chicken or beef

¹/4 to ¹/2 cup canola oil

4 cups shredded mixed red and green cabbage

3 cups fresh bean sprouts

3 (7-ounce) cans sliced water chestnuts, drained

2 green bell peppers, julienned

1 cup shredded carrots

8 ounces mushrooms, sliced

1 to 3 packages yakasoba noodles with seasoning packets

³/4 cup water

¹/2 to 1 cup Japanese Worcestershire sauce

Trim the pork and cut into strips. Heat 1 tablespoon of the canola oil in a wok or saucepan. Add the pork strips a few at a time and stir-fry until cooked through, adding additional canola oil as needed. Remove with a slotted spoon. Stir-fry the cabbage in additional canola oil just until tender-crisp; remove with a slotted spoon. Add the bean sprouts, water chestnuts, bell peppers, carrots and mushrooms with additional oil and stir-fry for 5 to 6 minutes or until tender; set aside.

Combine the noodles with the water in a large saucepan, reserving the seasoning packets. Cook until the noodles are loosened and the water is evaporated. Add the stir-fried pork and vegetables. Stir in the seasonings from the packets. Add the Worcestershire sauce and mix to coat well. Cook until heated through. Garnish the servings with dried seaweed.

NOTE: JAPANESE WORCESTERSHIRE SAUCE AND DRIED SEAWEED CAN BE FOUND AT ASIAN MARKETS.

Serves six

## Tucson Times

### ARIZONA BEDROOMS

Before the invention of air conditioning, Tucsonans would bed down outside! The legs of the beds were set in pans of water to deter spiders and scorpions. Some beds even had frames with canvas sides, which could be rolled down during summer rains.

# SAUSAGE AND RED PEPPER PASTA

1    pound sweet or
      hot sausage
2    tablespoons olive oil
1/2  teaspoon crumbled
      red pepper
1/2  cup chopped
      yellow onion
3    garlic cloves, chopped
1 1/2 cups heavy cream
1    (28-ounce) can plum
      tomatoes, drained,
      chopped
1/2  teaspoon salt
12  ounces uncooked bow
      tie pasta
Grated Parmesan cheese

Remove the sausage from the casings and crumble. Heat the olive oil in a saucepan. Add the sausage and red pepper. Cook for 7 to 10 minutes or until brown. Add the onion and garlic and cook until tender; drain. Stir in the cream and tomatoes. Cook until heated through. Season with the salt.

Cook the pasta using the package directions; drain. Combine with the sausage mixture in a serving bowl. Top with Parmesan cheese.

*Serves six to eight*

## Tucson Times

### PLANT PROTECTION

Cacti, agaves, ocotillos, desert trees, and certain other native Sonoran Desert plants are protected by law in Arizona and California. Taking the plants or cuttings from the wild requires a permit and the landowner's consent. A special tag is attached to each plant before it can be transported.

# FLYING BOW TIE PASTA

2    boneless skinless
     chicken breasts,
     cut into strips
2    tablespoons extra-virgin
     olive oil
2    garlic cloves, minced
4    ounces mushrooms,
     sliced
4    artichoke hearts,
     cut into wedges
2    tablespoons pine nuts
Salt and pepper to taste
1    tablespoon butter
$^1/_4$   cup white wine
$^1/_2$   cup chicken broth
12   ounces uncooked
     farfalle (bow tie pasta)
3    quarts water

Cook the chicken in 1 tablespoon of the olive oil in a skillet over high heat until light brown; remove with a slotted spoon. Add the remaining 1 tablespoon olive oil and heat over medium heat. Add the garlic and sauté until golden brown; discard the garlic.

Add the chicken, mushrooms, artichoke hearts and pine nuts to the skillet. Season with salt and pepper. Cook for 5 minutes. Stir in the butter, wine and chicken broth. Cook for 5 to 10 minutes or until slightly reduced.

Cook the pasta al dente in salted water in a saucepan; drain. Add to the chicken mixture and cook until heated through.

NOTE: YOU MAY GRILL THE CHICKEN IF PREFERRED.

Serves four

# ORZO WITH CHICKEN AND PEPPERS

### Pasta

2 (14-ounce) cans
   fat-free chicken broth
3/4 cup water
1 garlic clove, chopped
1 bay leaf
1 tablespoon each
   chopped fresh parsley
   and rosemary
1 cup white wine
1 1/2 cups uncooked orzo
Salt to taste

### Sauce

1/2 white onion, minced
1 teaspoon olive oil
1 1/2 to 2 pounds boneless
   skinless chicken breasts,
   cut into strips
2 garlic cloves, chopped
2 tablespoons each
   chopped fresh parsley,
   rosemary and basil
2 large red bell peppers,
   cut into strips
Salt and pepper to taste

*For the pasta*, combine the chicken broth, water, garlic, bay leaf, parsley and rosemary in a stockpot and simmer for 25 minutes. Add the wine and orzo and season with salt. Cook for 25 minutes or until the pasta is tender; discard the bay leaf.

*For the sauce*, sauté the onion in the olive oil in a skillet for 5 minutes or until translucent. Add the chicken and sauté until cooked through. Add the garlic, parsley, rosemary, basil and bell peppers. Sauté until the bell peppers are tender.

*To serve*, combine the pasta with the chicken sauce in a serving bowl and toss to mix well; season with salt and pepper. Garnish with a sprinkle of Parmesan cheese and tiny green peas around the edge of the bowl. Serve with a salad and French bread.

*Serves eight*

---

## About Thyme

### FINES HERBES

Fines herbes is a mixture of minced fresh chervil, chives, parsley, and tarragon. It may be used to season soups, savory sauces, and cheese and egg dishes.

# SESAME CHICKEN WITH CRISPY ANGEL HAIR PASTA

## Szechuan Sauce

| | |
|---|---|
| 2 | tablespoons sesame oil |
| 1/4 | tablespoon crushed red pepper |
| 1/4 | teaspoon Szechuan pepper |
| 1/4 | teaspoon ground ginger |
| 1 | tablespoon curry powder |
| 2 | garlic cloves, minced |
| 1/2 | teaspoon dry mustard |
| 1 | tablespoon red wine vinegar |
| 2 | tablespoons soy sauce |
| 2 | tablespoons brown sugar |
| 2 | cups chicken broth |

Cornstarch and dry sherry
Salt to taste

## Chicken

| | |
|---|---|
| 3 | pounds boneless skinless chicken breasts, cut into strips |

Flour for coating

| | |
|---|---|
| 2 | tablespoons sesame oil |
| 1 | red bell pepper, julienned |
| 3 or 4 | scallions, sliced diagonally |
| 8 | mushrooms, cut into quarters |

## Pasta

| | |
|---|---|
| 1/4 | cup sesame oil |
| 8 | ounces angel hair pasta, cooked, drained |

*For the sauce*, heat the sesame oil in a medium saucepan. Add the red pepper, Szechuan pepper, ginger, curry powder, garlic and dry mustard and sauté for 1 minute. Add the vinegar, soy sauce, brown sugar and chicken broth. Bring to a boil and reduce the heat. Simmer for 10 to 15 minutes.

Blend the cornstarch with enough sherry to coat a spoon in a bowl. Add to the sauce. Cook until thickened, stirring constantly. Add salt and adjust the seasonings.

*For the chicken*, coat the strips with flour. Sauté in the heated sesame oil in a wok or skillet until golden brown and cooked nearly through. Remove with a slotted spoon.

Add the bell pepper, scallions and mushrooms to the wok and sauté for several minutes. Add the chicken and sauce and mix well. Cook for several minutes until the chicken is cooked through.

*For the pasta*, heat the sesame oil in a large skillet until very hot. Spread the pasta evenly in the skillet. Cook until golden brown on both sides, turning once. Drain on a paper towel, patting dry.

*To serve*, place the pasta on serving plates. Spoon the chicken and sauce mixture over the pasta. Garnish with sesame seeds. Serve immediately.

NOTE: YOU MAY ADD OTHER VEGETABLES SUCH AS SNOW PEAS, CELERY OR BAMBOO SHOOTS.

*Serves four to six*

# SHRIMP AND ANGEL HAIR CASSEROLE

1  tablespoon butter
1  (9-ounce) package uncooked fresh angel hair pasta
1  (16-ounce) jar chunky mild salsa
1  pound medium shrimp, peeled, deveined
2  eggs, lightly beaten
1  cup half-and-half
1  cup plain yogurt
1/2  cup shredded Swiss cheese
1/3  cup crumbled feta cheese
1/3  cup chopped fresh parsley
1/4  cup chopped fresh basil, or 1 teaspoon dried basil leaves, crushed
1  teaspoon dried oregano leaves, crushed
1/2  cup shredded Monterey Jack cheese

Spread the butter over the bottom and sides of an 8 × 12-inch baking dish. Place half the pasta in the dish and spread with the salsa. Sprinkle with half the shrimp and top with the remaining pasta.

Combine the eggs, half-and-half, yogurt, Swiss cheese, feta cheese, parsley, basil and oregano in a medium bowl and mix well. Spread over the pasta layer in the baking dish and top with the remaining shrimp. Sprinkle with the Monterey Jack cheese.

Bake at 350 degrees for 30 minutes or until bubbly. Let stand for 10 minutes before serving.

*Serves six*

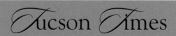

## Tucson Times

### SAGUAROS

Saguaros are a federally protected species of cactus that can reach fifty feet in height and two tons in weight, most of which is stored water. Many animals make the saguaro their home because the inside of the plant is twenty degrees cooler than the outside air.

# TEQUILA SHRIMP AND PASTA

24 large shrimp, peeled,
    deveined
3 garlic cloves, minced
1 tablespoon chopped
    cilantro
2 tablespoons olive oil
1 tablespoon lime juice
2 tablespoons tequila
2 tablespoons Triple Sec
16 ounces pasta, cooked,
    drained

Sauté the shrimp, garlic and cilantro in the heated olive oil in a skillet for 5 minutes. Stir in the lime juice, tequila and Triple Sec. Cook for 3 to 4 minutes longer or until the shrimp are no longer pink. Serve over the hot pasta.

*Serves four*

# ANYTIME PASTA

2 ounces prosciutto or
    pancetta, chopped
1/4 cup olive oil
1 tablespoon minced or
    puréed sun-dried
    tomatoes
2 tablespoons
    minced garlic
16 ounces pasta, cooked,
    drained
Grated Reggiano
    Parmigiano cheese

Sauté the prosciutto in the olive oil in a saucepan. Add the sun-dried tomatoes and garlic. Cook until heated through.

Spoon the hot pasta onto a serving platter or individual serving plates. Top with the prosciutto mixture. Sprinkle with grated cheese.

*Serves four*

# BASIL AND TOMATO
# PENNE WITH MOZZARELLA

6    garlic cloves, minced
1/2  cup olive oil
6 to 8 Roma tomatoes,
     chopped
1    teaspoon (scant) salt
1    bunch basil, julienned
16   ounces uncooked penne
Salt to taste
8    ounces fresh mozzarella
     cheese, cut
     into cubes

Sauté the garlic in the heated olive oil in a skillet until golden brown. Toss the tomatoes with 1 teaspoon salt in a small bowl. Add the garlic and oil mixture and mix well. Reserve a small amount of the basil for garnish and add the remaining basil to the tomato mixture; mix well.

Cook the pasta al dente in salted water using the package directions; drain. Add immediately to the tomato mixture with the cheese; toss to melt the cheese and mix well. Sprinkle with the reserved basil.

*Serves four*

# TOMATO SAUCE WITH PASTA

2    garlic cloves, chopped
2    tablespoons
     vegetable oil
1    medium onion, chopped
2    cups shredded carrots
1/2  cup shredded celery
1    (29-ounce) can
     crushed tomatoes
1    (8-ounce) can
     tomato sauce
1    tablespoon vinegar
2    tablespoons sugar
16   ounces pasta of choice
1    teaspoon salt
1    cup chopped
     fresh parsley
Grated Parmesan cheese
     to taste

Sauté the garlic in the oil in a large skillet for 3 minutes. Add the onion, carrots and celery. Sauté for 5 minutes. Stir in the tomatoes, tomato sauce, vinegar and sugar. Simmer for 40 minutes.

Cook the pasta in a large stockpot of boiling water with the salt until al dente; drain. Combine with 1/2 cup of the sauce in a large bowl and toss to mix. Divide among 4 plates. Add the parsley to the remaining sauce. Spoon over the pasta. Sprinkle with Parmesan cheese.

*Serves four*

# SAGUARO NATIONAL PARK

The majestic saguaro grows nowhere in the world except in certain areas of the Sonoran Desert. This giant cactus has become a symbol of the Southwest, and Saguaro National Park was established in 1933 as a monument to preserve lush stands of saguaros, their surrounding flora and fauna, and the rich history of the Hohokam who inhabited this region 300 to 1450 years ago.

With an average of only eleven inches of rain a year, desert plants grow slowly. The saguaro's growth is slowest at its seedling stage, taking as long as five years to reach only one inch above the ground. The arms, which give saguaros their characteristically human stance, take about seventy-five years to bud. Mature saguaros reaching forty feet in height can be up to 150 years old.

# LINGUINI WITH SWEET RED PEPPER SAUCE

4   red bell peppers, cut
     into strips
2   carrots, finely chopped
1   tablespoon olive oil
2   cups canned tomatoes
     in purée
$^1/_2$  pear, chopped
1   garlic clove, minced
1   tablespoon chopped
     fresh basil
1   tablespoon chopped
     fresh parsley
$^1/_8$  teaspoon red pepper
     flakes
Salt and black pepper
     to taste
16  ounces linguini,
     cooked, drained
2   tablespoons grated
     Parmesan cheese
2   tablespoons chopped
     fresh parsley

Sauté the bell peppers and carrots in the heated olive oil in a 10-inch skillet until tender. Add the tomatoes, pear, garlic, basil and 1 tablespoon parsley. Stir in the red pepper flakes, salt and black pepper. Simmer for 4 to 5 minutes to blend the flavors.

Spoon the pasta onto a serving plate or individual serving plates. Spoon the sauce over the pasta and sprinkle with the Parmesan cheese and 2 tablespoons parsley.

Serves six   

## Tucson Times

### TUCSON'S FIRST HOTELS

There were no hotels in Tucson in the 1850s. Some travelers slept in the corrals with the horses, but those well acquainted with Tucson's saloons had another option. A bartender at a cantina on Alameda Street occasionally rented out two cots in the back of the adobe building for overnight stays. Not exactly four-star lodging, but it was a start.

# ORECCHIETTE WITH TOMATO CREAM

1 (14-ounce) can juice-
  pack tomatoes, drained
1/2 cup heavy cream
1/2 cup milk
4 teaspoons tomato paste
1/8 to 1/4 teaspoon crushed
  red pepper flakes
Salt to taste
1 cup cooked peas
16 ounces orecchiette or
  bow tie pasta, cooked,
  drained
1/2 cup loosely packed
  julienned fresh basil

Chop the tomatoes. Combine the tomatoes, cream, milk, tomato paste, red pepper and salt in a 2-quart saucepan. Bring to a simmer over medium-low heat. Stir in the peas. Cook until heated through.

Add the pasta and toss to mix well. Sprinkle with the basil.

*Serves four*

# PENNE ALLA NAPOLITANA

12 ounces uncooked penne
1 tablespoon virgin
  olive oil
2 tablespoons
  minced garlic
3 tablespoons virgin
  olive oil
2 cups tomato sauce
1 cup sliced black olives
1/4 cup coarsely chopped
  fresh basil
1 teaspoon red
  pepper flakes
1/2 cup (1/4-inch)
  mozzarella cheese cubes
1/2 cup grated Parmesan
  cheese

Cook the pasta using the package directions. Drain the pasta and toss with 1 tablespoon olive oil; keep warm.

Sauté the garlic in 3 tablespoons heated olive oil in a medium skillet over medium-high heat until light brown. Stir in the tomato sauce, olives, basil and red pepper flakes. Cook until heated through, stirring occasionally.

Add the mozzarella cheese and Parmesan cheese and stir until the cheeses melt. Serve over the hot pasta, tossing to coat well. Serve with additional Parmesan cheese if desired.

*Serves four*

# PASTA WITH PEPPER SAUCE

2 medium onions, thinly
sliced
2 or 3 red bell peppers,
sliced $1/2$ inch thick
1 or 2 hot red chiles, sliced
$1/4$ cup grapeseed oil
2 tablespoons chopped
fresh basil, or
1 tablespoon dried basil
Salt and freshly ground
black pepper to taste
1 cup reduced-sodium
chicken broth
16 ounces uncooked penne
or farfalle
$1/2$ cup reduced-sodium
chicken broth
(optional)
1 to 2 tablespoons extra-
virgin olive oil
1 to 2 tablespoons finely
chopped Italian parsley
$1/2$ cup grated Parmesan
cheese

Sauté the onions, bell peppers and chiles in the heated grapeseed oil in a large skillet over high heat until the onions begin to brown. Reduce the heat and add the basil, salt and black pepper. Simmer for 15 minutes or until the peppers are tender. Add 1 cup chicken broth and cook for several minutes longer.

Cook the pasta al dente in boiling salted water in a saucepan; keep warm.

Reserve 8 to 10 slices of the bell peppers. Process the remaining pepper mixture in a food processor, adding chicken broth if needed to produce the consistency of thick tomato sauce.

Drain the hot pasta and toss with the pepper sauce. Spoon onto serving plates and drizzle with the olive oil. Top with the reserved bell pepper slices, parsley and cheese.

*Serves four to six*

## Cooking Tips

### HOLDING PASTA

To hold pasta for later use, add one tablespoon olive oil to the cooking water. Drain the pasta, place on a platter, and cover with a warm damp paper towel.

# PENNE WITH ASPARAGUS AND PINE NUTS

1   *pound fresh asparagus,*
    *trimmed*
8   *ounces uncooked penne*
2   *tablespoons olive oil*
1   *cup chopped roasted red*
    *bell pepper*
1/4  *cup grated lemon zest*
1/4  *cup fresh lemon juice*
6   *tablespoons toasted*
    *pine nuts*
*Salt and pepper to taste*
6   *tablespoons shaved*
    *Parmesan cheese*

Steam the asparagus for 3 to 4 minutes or until tender; drain and cut into 1-inch pieces.

Cook the pasta using the package directions; drain. Combine with the olive oil in a large serving bowl and toss to coat well. Add the asparagus, roasted bell pepper, lemon zest, lemon juice, pine nuts, salt and pepper and toss to mix well. Add the cheese and toss again.

*Serves four*   

# PASTA WITH SUNFLOWER KERNELS

3   *sprigs of parsley,*
    *chopped*
3   *garlic cloves, minced*
1   *teaspoon grated*
    *lemon zest*
1/2  *cup sunflower oil*
1/2  *teaspoon salt*
1/2  *teaspoon pepper*
8   *ounces tomato, spinach*
    *or plain spaghetti,*
    *cooked, drained*
2/3  *cup grated Parmesan*
    *cheese*
1/2  *cup roasted sunflower*
    *kernels*

Sauté the parsley, garlic and lemon zest in the heated sunflower oil in a small skillet over medium-high heat for 1 minute. Season with salt and pepper.

Combine with the pasta in a serving bowl. Add the cheese and sunflower kernels; toss to mix well.

*Serves four*

# HOMEMADE SPINACH AND GARLIC PASTA

**Homemade Pasta**

| | |
|---|---|
| 8 | ounces fresh spinach |
| 6 | large garlic cloves, crushed, finely chopped |
| $^1/_2$ | teaspoon salt |
| $1^1/_2$ | cups flour |
| 2 | eggs |
| 4 | egg yolks |
| 1 | teaspoon olive oil |

**Onion Pasta Sauce**

| | |
|---|---|
| 1 | pound Vidalia or other sweet onions, thinly sliced |
| 12 | garlic cloves, chopped |
| $^1/_2$ | cup (1 stick) butter |
| 1 | teaspoon olive oil |
| 1 | teaspoon honey |
| $^1/_3$ | cup marsala |

*To make the pasta,* blanch the spinach. Drain the spinach, press to remove the excess moisture and finely chop. Combine with the garlic and salt in a bowl and mix well.

Place 1 cup of the flour in a large stainless steel mixing bowl and make a well in the center. Add the eggs, egg yolks, olive oil and spinach mixture to the well. Mix well, adding additional flour as needed to form a dough.

Knead the dough on a floured surface until smooth. Let rest for several minutes. Roll the dough as desired in a pasta machine, using the manufacturer's instructions. Cut to desired width.

*For the sauce,* cook the onions and garlic in the melted butter and olive oil in a covered skillet over medium heat until tender. Add the honey and reduce the heat. Simmer for 30 minutes. Add the wine and simmer for 5 to 10 minutes longer.

*To finish the dish,* cook the pasta in boiling water in a saucepan for 2 minutes or until tender; drain. Toss with the sauce in a bowl. Garnish with grated Parmesan cheese.

*Serves two to four*

# SUMMER SPAGHETTI

1    pound firm plum
     tomatoes, coarsely
     chopped
1    medium onion, chopped
6    green olives, chopped
2    medium garlic cloves,
     chopped
1/3  cup chopped fresh
     parsley
1/3  cup chopped fresh basil
2    tablespoons drained
     capers
1/2  teaspoon paprika
1/4  teaspoon dried oregano
     leaves, crumbled
1    tablespoon red wine
     vinegar
1/2  cup olive oil
16   ounces uncooked
     (number 10) spaghetti

Combine the tomatoes, onion, olives, garlic, parsley, basil, capers, paprika and oregano in a glass bowl and toss to mix well. Drizzle with the vinegar and then with the olive oil; mix well. Chill, covered, in the refrigerator for 6 to 10 hours.

Cook the spaghetti in boiling water in a saucepan for 8 to 10 minutes or until al dente; drain.

Combine the hot pasta with the chilled sauce in a bowl and toss to mix well. Serve immediately.

*Serves four to six*

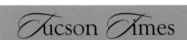

## PIMA AIR AND SPACE MUSEUM

Pima Air and Space Museum is the largest privately funded museum in the world. It has more than two hundred examples of nearly every type of flying machine ever invented. There is a perfect replica of the Wright Flyer, an SR-71, presidential airplanes, world war bombers, and helicopters.

# Rigatoni with
# White Beans and Tomatoes

6   *tablespoons olive oil*
3   *garlic cloves, minced*
20  *fresh sage leaves*
1¼ *pounds plum tomatoes,*
    *peeled, chopped*
*Salt and pepper to taste*
2   *(15-ounce) cans*
    *cannellini*
16  *ounces uncooked*
    *rigatoni*

Heat the olive oil in a large saucepan. Add the garlic and sage and sauté until the garlic is translucent. Add the tomatoes, salt and pepper. Simmer for 20 minutes. Add the beans. Simmer, partially covered, for 15 minutes.

Cook the pasta al dente using the package directions; drain. Add to the saucepan and toss to mix well.

*Serves six*

## Other Temptations

### Pasta Puttanesca

This version of pasta is named for the ladies of evening because the sauce has such a siren call. For an easy version, sauté chopped onions, minced garlic, drained canned artichoke hearts and olives in olive oil in a skillet until tender. Add undrained reconstituted sun-dried tomatoes. Toss with drained cooked pasta and serve. You may vary the amounts of the ingredients to suit your taste, but the dish is best made in quantities to serve no more than six.

# ROTINI WITH MUSHROOM CABERNET SAUCE

1    cup chopped porcini,
     shiitake or portobello
     mushrooms
2    garlic cloves, minced
Cayenne pepper to taste
1    tablespoon olive oil
3    cups drained chopped
     tomatoes
1/4  cup cabernet sauvignon
2    teaspoons salt
10   ounces rotini, cooked,
     drained

Sauté the mushrooms, garlic and cayenne pepper in the olive oil in a skillet until the mushrooms begin to be tender. Add the tomatoes, wine and salt and cook until thickened to sauce consistency. Toss with the pasta in a serving bowl.

*Serves four*

# SPAGHETTI WITH CHICK-PEA SAUCE

1    small onion, chopped
1/2  cup olive oil
3    garlic cloves, minced
1/4  cup chopped fresh
     parsley
1/2  teaspoon dried
     marjoram
1/2  teaspoon dried oregano
1/4  teaspoon red
     pepper flakes
1 1/4 cups drained canned
     chick-peas
Salt to taste
16   ounces spaghetti,
     cooked al dente,
     drained
1/2  cup grated Parmesan
     cheese

Sauté the onion in the heated olive oil in a medium saucepan until tender. Add the garlic and sauté for 1 minute. Stir in the parsley, marjoram, oregano and pepper flakes and cook for 1 minute. Add the chick-peas and salt. Cook until heated through. Add the pasta and cheese and toss to coat well.

*Serves four*

# SUN-DRIED TOMATO AND MUSHROOM FETTUCCINI

16 ounces uncooked
    fettuccini
Salt to taste
8 ounces mixed cultivated
    and wild mushrooms,
    thinly sliced
2 large garlic cloves,
    chopped
1 tablespoon butter
1/2 teaspoon dried tarragon
    leaves, crumbled
1 cup oil-pack sun-dried
    tomatoes
1/2 cup heavy cream
1 1/2 tablespoons madeira
1 cup grated Parmesan
    cheese
Pepper to taste

Cook the pasta al dente in boiling salted water in a large saucepan; keep warm.

Sauté the mushrooms and garlic in the melted butter in a heavy medium skillet over medium-low heat for 5 minutes or until nearly tender. Add the tarragon and sauté for 2 minutes or until the mushrooms release their juices. Stir in the sun-dried tomatoes, cream and wine. Simmer for 1 minute or just until the flavors blend.

Drain the pasta and add to the sauce with the cheese. Season with salt and pepper and toss to coat well. Garnish servings with chopped fresh parsley.

*Serves four*

## Cooking Tips

### DRIED TOMATOES

Tomatoes dried in the sun are usually labeled sun-dried; those dried in a dehydrator are simply called dried tomatoes. Both have an intense and sweet tomato taste, but sun-dried tomatoes often taste saltier because salt is used in the sun-drying process. They may be packed dry or in oil. Keep dry forms in an airtight container in the refrigerator, or in the freezer for storage for up to one year. Oil-pack tomatoes will keep in the refrigerator for up to six months after opening if the oil covers the tomatoes.

# Winter Greens Puttanesca

2  red or yellow
   bell peppers
6  cups fresh spinach or
   arugula, trimmed
1  large garlic clove,
   minced
Freshly ground pepper
   to taste
1  cup pitted green or
   black olives
1  (2-ounce) can
   anchovies, drained,
   cut into halves
   crosswise
1/3  cup extra-virgin
   olive oil
8  ounces uncooked
   rigatoni or other
   wide-tube pasta
Salt to taste

Cut the bell peppers into halves and discard the membranes and seeds. Place the peppers skin side up on a foil-lined baking sheet and press to flatten slightly. Broil 3 inches from the heat source until the skins are charred. Steam in a sealed paper bag for 15 minutes and slip off the skins. Cut into 1/4-inch strips.

Combine the spinach and garlic in a large bowl and season generously with the pepper. Add the roasted peppers and olives and toss to mix. Add the anchovies and drizzle with the olive oil; toss to coat well.

Cook the pasta al dente in salted boiling water in a large saucepan; rinse and drain. Add to the spinach mixture and toss. Garnish with coarsely grated Parmesan cheese.

*Serves six*

# Temptations à la Carte

## SIDE DISHES

## ACTIVE FARE

One of the most popular athletic events in southern Arizona is
the El Tour de Tucson. Thousands of cyclists from across the country
participate in the tour with routes of 111, 75, 50, and 25 miles.
This annual November event is one of America's ten best century rides.
Though the cyclists may prefer a long soak in the bathtub,
the spectators would award this fare.

## Menu

MUSHROOMS STUFFED
WITH SUN-DRIED TOMATOES

TUSCAN TENDERLOIN

TARRAGON SHERRY CARROTS

GREEK-STYLE GREEN BEANS

LEMON ICE

GUILT-FREE CHOCOLATE CAKE

# GREEK-STYLE GREEN BEANS

4 medium white onions, chopped
3 garlic cloves, crushed
1 tablespoon olive oil
4 large tomatoes, peeled, sliced
Pepper to taste
2 pounds fresh green beans, trimmed
Salt to taste

Sauté the onions and garlic in the olive oil in a skillet until light brown. Add the tomatoes and season with pepper.

Cook the beans in salted water in a saucepan for 5 minutes; drain. Add the tomato mixture and cover. Simmer for 30 to 60 minutes or until done to taste, removing the cover toward the end of the cooking time. Adjust the seasonings.

Serves six

## Other Temptations

### ASPARAGUS WITH MUSHROOMS AND FRESH CILANTRO

Trim 1 pound fresh asparagus and slice diagonally into 1-inch pieces. Sauté 2 cups sliced mushrooms in 2 tablespoons melted butter or margarine in a skillet over high heat until light brown. Add the asparagus. Sauté for 1 minute. Add 2 tablespoons chopped shallots, 1/2 teaspoon salt and 1 teaspoon freshly ground pepper. Sprinkle with 1/4 cup chopped cilantro and sauté for 30 seconds longer.

# HEARTLAND HARVEST GREEN BEANS

6   *medium carrots*
7   *slices bacon*
2   *(9-ounce) packages frozen whole green beans, thawed or 18 ounces fresh green beans*
2   *garlic cloves, minced*
2   *tablespoons butter*
1/2 *teaspoon pepper*
*Garlic salt to taste*

Julienne the carrots into 3- to 4-inch-long strips. Cook the bacon in a large skillet over medium heat for 8 to 10 minutes or until crisp, turning occasionally. Remove the bacon and place on paper towels to drain, reserving the drippings. Crumble the bacon into a small bowl and set aside.

Sauté the green beans, carrots and garlic in the butter and 2 tablespoons of the reserved bacon drippings in the skillet over medium heat for 5 minutes or until the vegetables are tender-crisp. Stir in the pepper and garlic salt. Spoon into a serving bowl. Top with the crumbled bacon.

*Serves eight*

# BROCCOLI WITH LEMON AND GARLIC

2   *large heads broccoli*
4   *garlic cloves, chopped*
2   *tablespoons light olive oil*
1/2 *cup water or chicken stock*
*Salt and freshly ground pepper to taste*
*Juice of 1 lemon*
1/2 *teaspoon grated lemon zest (optional)*

Cut the heads of the broccoli into florets and cut the tender portions of the stems into thin slices. Rinse and drain well.

Stir-fry the garlic in the olive oil in a skillet over medium-high heat until tender; remove with a slotted spoon. Increase the heat to high and add the broccoli. Stir-fry for 2 minutes.

Stir in the water. Cook, covered, for 2 to 3 minutes or until the broccoli is tender. Cook, uncovered, until the liquid evaporates. Season with salt and pepper and stir in the garlic and lemon juice. Sprinkle with the lemon zest.

*Serves eight*

# LEMON-MUSTARD BRUSSELS SPROUTS

3   tablespoons fresh
    lemon juice
1¹/2 tablespoons whole-grain
    mustard
1¹/2 pounds Brussels sprouts
1   teaspoon salt
3   tablespoons olive oil
Salt and freshly ground
    pepper to taste

Mix the lemon juice and mustard in a bowl. Trim the Brussels sprouts and cut into halves lengthwise.

Combine the Brussels sprouts with 1 teaspoon salt and water to cover in a large saucepan. Cook for 2 to 3 minutes or until tender-crisp; drain and cool to room temperature.

Heat the olive oil in a large wok or skillet over medium-high heat. Add the Brussels sprouts and stir-fry for 1 to 2 minutes or just until golden brown. Season with salt and pepper to taste. Combine with the lemon and mustard mixture in a bowl and mix gently. Serve immediately.

Serves six

# TARRAGON SHERRY CARROTS

1¹/2 pounds carrots
¹/2  cup water
1   teaspoon tarragon
¹/2  cup chopped onion
2   tablespoons butter
3   tablespoons flour
³/4  cup evaporated milk
¹/3  cup sherry

Peel the carrots and cut into 3-inch julienne strips to measure about 4 cups. Combine with the water and tarragon in a medium saucepan. Cook, covered, over medium-low heat for 10 minutes or until tender-crisp; do not drain.

Sauté the onion in the butter in a large saucepan. Stir in the flour and cook until bubbly. Stir in the evaporated milk and wine gradually. Add the undrained carrots and cook until the mixture thickens, stirring constantly.

Serves eight

# BROWN SUGAR-GLAZED CARROTS

1¹/2 pounds carrots
Salt to taste
2 tablespoons margarine
  or butter
¹/3 cup packed brown
  sugar
¹/2 teaspoon salt
¹/2 teaspoon grated
  orange zest

Peel the carrots and cut into strips lengthwise. Add to salted boiling water in a saucepan and cover. Bring to a boil and cook for 18 to 20 minutes or until tender; drain.

Melt the margarine in a 12-inch skillet. Stir in the brown sugar, ¹/2 teaspoon salt and orange zest. Cook until bubbly, stirring constantly. Add the carrots and cook for 5 minutes or until the carrots are glazed, stirring occasionally.

*Serves five or six*

## Other Temptations

### HONEY-BAKED ONIONS

Slice 6 large onions and arrange the slices in a greased 9 × 13-inch baking dish. Drizzle with 1 tablespoon lemon juice and 4 drops of Tabasco sauce. Melt ¹/4 cup butter with ¹/3 cup honey and ¹/2 teaspoon salt in a small saucepan. Pour over the onions. Bake at 425 degrees for 45 minutes or until the onions are tender and golden brown. Serve with pork roast.

# CAULIFLOWER CRÈME FRAÎCHE

1 (3-pound) head
  cauliflower
2 tablespoons unsalted
  butter
2 tablespoons
  unbleached flour
1 cup milk
1 cup crème fraîche
2 ounces chévre cheese,
  crumbled
1/4 cup chopped
  fresh chives
Salt, cayenne pepper and
  freshly ground black
  pepper to taste

Trim the cauliflower and break into florets. Add to a large saucepan of boiling water and reduce the heat. Simmer for 10 minutes or until fork-tender; drain. Place in a lightly buttered 12-inch gratin dish or shallow baking dish.

Melt the butter in a small saucepan and whisk in the flour. Cook until smooth, stirring constantly. Add the milk gradually and cook until thickened, stirring constantly. Stir in the crème fraîche, cheese, chives, salt, cayenne pepper and black pepper.

Pour the sauce over the cauliflower. Bake at 350 degrees for 40 minutes or until bubbly and golden brown.

*Serves six*

## Other Temptations

### CRÈME FRAÎCHE

Crème fraîche has a slightly tangy nutty flavor and can be used as a topping for vegetables as well as desserts. It can also be used as a garnish for soups or a thickener for salad dressings. It can be found at most supermarkets, but to make crème fraîche, bring 2 cups heavy cream and 1/2 cup sour cream to room temperature and combine in a bowl. Whisk until smooth and cover with plastic wrap. Let stand in a warm place for 12 hours or longer. Store, covered, in the refrigerator for up to 2 weeks.

# CORN CASSEROLE WITH GREEN CHILES

1   (16-ounce) package
    frozen corn
1   (16-ounce) can cream-
    style corn
1   (7-ounce) package corn
    muffin mix
1/2  (4-ounce) can chopped
    green chiles
1/4  cup (1/2 stick) butter,
    melted
2   eggs, lightly beaten
1   cup sour cream
1   cup shredded
    Cheddar cheese

Combine the frozen corn, cream-style corn, corn muffin mix and chiles in a bowl. Stir in the melted butter and eggs. Fold in the sour cream. Spoon into a buttered 9 × 13-inch baking dish and sprinkle with the cheese. Bake at 350 degrees for 35 minutes or until a knife comes out clean.

NOTE: YOU MAY OMIT THE GREEN CHILES IF DESIRED.

*Serves six to eight*

# CARAMELIZED CORN WITH PUMPKIN SEEDS

1   cup frozen corn kernels
2   tablespoons olive oil
Salt and pepper to taste
1/4  cup pumpkin seeds
1/4  cup chopped cilantro
1/4  cup chopped fresh or
    roasted red bell pepper
1/4  cup chopped
    green chiles
Juice of 1 lime

Cook the corn in the olive oil in a skillet until medium brown; drain. Season with salt and pepper. Add the pumpkin seeds, cilantro, bell pepper, chiles and lime juice and mix well. Serve at room temperature.

NOTE: THIS MAY BE SERVED AS A SALAD AS WELL AS A SIDE DISH.

*Serves four*

# MEDITERRANEAN STUFFED EGGPLANT

2   (1-pound) eggplant
Salt to taste
1   cup minced ham or veal
2   tablespoons olive oil
1   cup chopped red
    Spanish onion
2   garlic cloves, cut
    into halves
4   tomatoes, thinly sliced
2   cups vegetable stock
1   cup arborio or other
    short grain rice
1   teaspoon dried
    marjoram
1   teaspoon dried thyme
Freshly ground pepper
    to taste
2   tablespoons olive oil
2   tablespoons chopped
    fresh parsley

Cut the eggplant into halves lengthwise. Sprinkle with salt and place cut side down in a colander. Let drain for 30 minutes.

Sauté the ham in 2 tablespoons heated olive oil in a large skillet over medium heat for 3 to 4 minutes. Add the onion and garlic and sauté for 2 to 3 minutes or until the onion is tender. Add half the sliced tomatoes and $1/2$ cup of the vegetable stock. Simmer, covered, for 5 minutes.

Rinse the eggplant under cold water. Scoop out the pulp, leaving shells 1 inch thick; reserve the shells and pulp.

Chop the reserved pulp coarsely and add to the ham mixture with the rice, marjoram, thyme and 1 cup vegetable stock. Simmer, covered, over medium heat for 15 minutes, stirring occasionally. Discard the garlic halves and season with salt and pepper.

Spoon the ham mixture into the reserved eggplant shells and arrange in a baking dish. Drizzle 2 tablespoons olive oil around the eggplant. Place the remaining tomato slices around the eggplant and add the remaining $1/2$ cup vegetable stock.

Bake at 350 degrees for 40 to 45 minutes or until tender, mashing the tomatoes with a spoon and basting the eggplant during the baking time. Remove to a serving platter and sprinkle with the parsley. Spoon the sauce from the baking dish over the top.

NOTE: THIS CAN ALSO BE SERVED AS A LIGHT MAIN DISH.

Serves four

# BAKED MUSHROOMS

3 pounds small fresh
  mushrooms
1 small onion, chopped
$^1/_2$ cup (1 stick) butter or
  margarine
$^1/_2$ cup flour
$^1/_4$ teaspoon garlic powder
$^3/_4$ teaspoon salt
$^1/_8$ teaspoon pepper
$2^1/_2$ cups chicken stock
1 cup sour cream
1 tablespoon tomato
  sauce
1 tablespoon sherry

Sauté the mushrooms and onion in batches in half the butter in a skillet for 5 minutes; remove to a 2-quart baking dish.

Melt the remaining butter in the skillet. Stir in the flour, garlic powder, salt and pepper. Cook until bubbly. Add the chicken stock, sour cream, tomato sauce and wine. Cook until thickened, stirring constantly.

Pour over the mushrooms in the baking dish. Bake, covered, at 350 for 30 minutes or until bubbly.

*Serves eight*

## Cooking Tips

### ABOUT MUSHROOMS

There are many kinds of cultivated and wild mushrooms on the market today. They need to be fresh, so buy them no more than a few days before their intended use. Select firm mushrooms that are evenly colored with tightly closed caps. Clean mushrooms just before using by wiping with a damp paper towel. Mushrooms are very absorbent and may become mushy if immersed in water.

# STUFFED RED PEPPERS

**Tomato Sauce**

- 1    medium onion, chopped
- 2    tablespoons olive oil
- 1    garlic clove, minced
- 1    (16-ounce) can Italian tomatoes
- 2 to 3 tablespoons chopped fresh basil
- Salt and pepper to taste

**Peppers**

- 3    large red bell peppers
- Salt to taste
- 12   ounces stemmed spinach leaves
- 16   ounces ricotta cheese
- 2    eggs
- 3    tablespoons soft bread crumbs
- 1/2  cup shredded Swiss cheese
- 1/2  cup grated Parmesan cheese
- 1/4  teaspoon freshly grated nutmeg
- 1/4  teaspoon salt
- 1/2  teaspoon freshly ground pepper
- 1/4  cup grated Parmesan cheese

*For the sauce,* sauté the onion in the heated olive oil in a small saucepan just until tender. Add the garlic and sauté lightly. Add the undrained tomatoes, basil, salt and pepper. Simmer for 10 to 15 minutes or until thickened to the desired consistency, stirring frequently.

*For the peppers,* cut the bell peppers into halves, discarding the stems, membranes and seeds. Blanch in boiling salted water in a saucepan for 5 minutes or just until tender-crisp. Drain and rinse under cold water.

Steam the spinach for 3 minutes or until wilted. Drain, rinse under cold water and press to remove excess moisture. Chop coarsely.

Combine the ricotta cheese, eggs and bread crumbs in a large bowl and mix well. Stir in the spinach, Swiss cheese, 1/2 cup Parmesan cheese, nutmeg, salt and pepper.

*To assemble,* spread 1/2 cup of the sauce in a shallow baking dish. Arrange the pepper halves cut side up in the prepared dish and spoon 1 tablespoon of the sauce into each pepper. Spoon some of the spinach mixture into each pepper and top with the remaining sauce.

Sprinkle with 1/4 cup Parmesan cheese. Bake at 400 degrees for 30 minutes or until the spinach mixture is set and the tops are golden brown.

NOTE: SERVE AS A SIDE DISH OR A MEATLESS MAIN DISH.

*Serves six*

# BASQUE POTATOES

6     tablespoons ($^3$/4 stick)
      unsalted butter
3     tablespoons olive oil
3     garlic cloves, chopped
$^1$/2   cup chopped fresh
      parsley
1     tablespoon dried
      rosemary, crushed
$^1$/2   teaspoon dried thyme
1$^1$/2 teaspoons paprika
$^1$/2   teaspoon salt
$^1$/4   teaspoon pepper
3     pounds small new white
      or red potatoes

Combine the butter, olive oil, garlic, parsley, rosemary, thyme, paprika, salt and pepper in a Dutch oven. Cook on the stove top until the butter melts, stirring to mix well.

Add the potatoes and turn to coat well. Bake at 375 degrees for 40 minutes, turning the potatoes frequently to prevent sticking.

*Serves six*

## About Thyme

### THYME TENDENCIES

In addition to vegetables, thyme is good in any slowly cooked dish such as soups and stews because it withstands a long cooking time well, providing a background note that blends well with other flavors. Use it also in tomato-based sauces, roasted poultry, broiled or roasted meats, and even breads.

# CRAB-STUFFED POTATOES

4    large baking potatoes
2    tablespoons butter
1/3   cup half-and-half
1/2   cup shredded
      mozzarella cheese
3    ounces cream cheese,
      softened
4    ounces cooked crab
      meat, flaked
1    tablespoon minced
      green onions
1/4   teaspoon nutmeg
1/4   teaspoon salt
Pepper to taste
Melted butter
Paprika and chopped parsley
      to taste

Pierce the potatoes and bake at 425 degrees for 45 minutes or until tender. Cut a thin lengthwise slice from each potato and scoop out the pulp, leaving 1/4-inch shells.

Combine the potato pulp with 2 tablespoons butter, half-and-half, mozzarella cheese, cream cheese, crab meat, green onions, nutmeg, salt and pepper in a mixing bowl and beat until smooth.

Spoon the crab meat mixture into the potatoes, packing lightly. Place on a baking sheet and drizzle with the melted butter. Sprinkle with paprika and parsley. Bake at 400 degrees for 20 minutes or until heated through.

*Serves four*

# FORT LOWELL MUSEUM

The U.S. Army's original Camp Lowell was built in 1866 near present-day downtown Tucson.
In 1873 it was relocated seven miles northeast of the original site, near the Rillito and Pantano Wash.
As was the custom of the day, a row of cottonwood trees was planted in front of the
officers' quarters. In 1877 the fort was given permanent status and became the place to be stationed.
By 1891 the Apache threat was over and the fort was abandoned. The gardens withered,
the cottonwoods died, and most of the adobe structures were lost to the elements. The Junior League of
Tucson was instrumental in saving Fort Lowell by raising funds to open the museum building, which
is an accurate reconstruction of the commanding officer's quarters with rooms decorated in period style.

# LEMON BASIL POTATO PUFF

| | |
|---|---|
| 2 | pounds potatoes |
| 3/4 | cup fine dry bread crumbs |
| 3 | tablespoons butter or margarine, melted |
| 1 | tablespoon finely chopped fresh parsley |
| 3 | egg yolks, lightly beaten |
| 1 | teaspoon grated lemon zest |
| 1 | teaspoon lemon juice |
| 1/4 | cup chopped fresh basil or lemon basil |
| 3/4 | teaspoon salt |
| 1/4 | teaspoon white pepper |
| 1 | cup milk |
| 1 | cup shredded Swiss cheese |
| 3 | egg whites |
| 1/2 | cup shredded Swiss cheese |

Peel the potatoes and cut into quarters. Cook in water to cover in a large saucepan for 20 to 25 minutes or until tender; drain. Mash the potatoes until smooth.

Combine the bread crumbs, butter and parsley in a bowl and mix well. Press over the bottom and sides of a lightly greased 1$\frac{1}{2}$-quart baking dish.

Combine the egg yolks, lemon zest, lemon juice, basil, salt and white pepper in a bowl and mix well. Stir in the milk and 1 cup cheese. Add to the potatoes and mix well.

Beat the egg whites in a mixing bowl until stiff peaks form. Fold into the potato mixture. Spoon the potatoes into the prepared baking dish. Top with 1/2 cup cheese.

Bake at 350 degrees for 45 minutes or until a knife inserted in the center comes out clean. Garnish with chopped parsley.

Serves six

# MASHED POTATOES WITH
# CARAMELIZED ONIONS

2   (8-ounce) sweet onions
1/4  cup (1/2 stick) unsalted
     butter, melted
1/4  cup chardonnay
6    russet potatoes, about
     2 1/2 pounds
Salt to taste
1/4  cup (1/2 stick) unsalted
     butter
1/2  cup (about) milk
Freshly ground pepper

Cut the onions into halves crosswise and slice thinly. Combine with 1/4 cup melted butter in a sauté pan over medium heat. Cook for 10 minutes or until the onions begin to brown, stirring occasionally. Reduce the heat and stir in the wine. Cook for 20 minutes longer or until golden brown, stirring frequently.

Peel the potatoes and cut into quarters. Cook in lightly salted water to cover in a saucepan until tender; drain and return to the saucepan. Mash with 1/4 cup butter and enough milk to make of the desired consistency. Season with salt and pepper.

Add the onions and mix well. Adjust the seasonings and butter. Serve hot.

*Serves eight*

## Other Temptations

### POTATO AND CARROT GRATIN

Cook and mash 6 peeled medium potatoes and 1 pound peeled carrots. Combine with 1 cup sour cream, 1 egg, 1 1/2 cups shredded Cheddar cheese, 1 1/2 tablespoons prepared mustard, 1 tablespoon butter and salt and pepper to taste in a bowl and mix well. Spoon into a baking dish and bake at 350 degrees for 20 minutes.

# Scalloped Potatoes and Mushrooms

4   medium potatoes
1   pound fresh mushrooms
2   teaspoons vegetable oil
1   tablespoon flour
1/4  teaspoon salt
1/4  teaspoon pepper
1/2  cup grated Parmesan
    cheese
3   tablespoons butter or
    margarine
3/4  cup low-fat milk
1   tablespoon chopped
    parsley

Cut the potatoes into 1/8-inch slices and combine with water 2 inches deep in a 2-quart saucepan. Cook, covered, over medium heat for 6 to 8 minutes or until nearly tender; drain.

Cut the mushrooms into 1/4-inch slices. Sauté in the heated oil in a large nonstick skillet over medium heat until the mushrooms are tender and the liquid evaporates.

Combine the flour, salt and pepper in a small bowl. Spray a shallow 11/2-quart baking dish with nonstick cooking spray.

Alternate layers of the potatoes, a sprinkle of the flour mixture, mushrooms, cheese and dots of butter until all the ingredients are used and ending with the butter. Pour the milk over the layers.

Bake at 400 degrees for 30 minutes or until the potatoes are tender and the top is golden brown. Sprinkle with the parsley.

*Serves four*

## Tucson Times

### Arizona Birds

The Sonoran Desert has about 300 species of birds, more than any other arid region in the world, making Tucson a favorite spot for bird watching. The roadrunner, a member of the cuckoo family, is native to the area. It is the fastest American bird afoot, traveling 15 miles per hour or more when fleeing its predators.

# THYME POTATOES

3    pounds potatoes
1/2  medium onion, chopped
1/2  cup (or more) olive oil
2    tablespoons butter
1    tablespoon red wine
     vinegar
1    teaspoon dried thyme
1/4  teaspoon garlic powder
Salt and pepper to taste

Cook the potatoes in water to cover in a saucepan until tender; drain. Sauté the onion in 1/2 cup olive oil and butter in a skillet until tender. Add the vinegar, thyme, garlic powder, salt and pepper and mix well. Chop the potatoes and combine with the onion mixture in a serving bowl, adding additional olive oil if necessary to coat well.

*Serves four*

# SUNBELT SPINACH

2    tablespoons chopped
     onion
2    garlic cloves,
     finely chopped
2    tablespoons olive oil
1 1/2 pounds fresh spinach,
     trimmed
1/4  cup raisins or
     chopped dates
Ground nutmeg, salt and
     pepper to taste
1/4  cup toasted pine nuts

Sauté the onion and garlic in the heated olive oil in a large skillet over medium-high heat until tender. Add the spinach and sauté for 5 to 6 minutes or until tender. Stir in the raisins, nutmeg, salt and pepper. Sprinkle with the pine nuts.

*Serves four*

# SPICED BUTTERNUT SQUASH

1   (2-pound) butternut
    squash
1   teaspoon minced garlic
2   tablespoons
    vegetable oil
1   teaspoon sesame oil
1/3  cup chicken broth
1/4  cup dry white wine
2   teaspoons minced
    gingerroot
1 1/2 teaspoons minced garlic
1/4  teaspoon five-spice
    powder
1/8  teaspoon cayenne
    pepper
Salt and black pepper
    to taste

Peel the squash and cut into 1-inch pieces, discarding the seeds. Sauté with 1 teaspoon garlic in the heated vegetable oil and sesame oil in a large skillet over medium heat for 8 minutes or until the squash is tender-crisp.

Add the chicken broth and wine. Cook for 8 minutes or until most of the liquid has evaporated. Stir in the gingerroot, 1 1/2 teaspoons garlic, five-spice powder and cayenne pepper. Reduce the heat and simmer, covered, for 5 minutes or until the liquid has evaporated. Season with salt and black pepper.

*Serves four*

---

## Other Temptations

### BROILED BALSAMIC EGGPLANT

Whisk together 1/2 cup balsamic vinegar, 1/4 cup olive oil, 2 finely chopped scallions and salt and pepper to taste in a shallow ovenproof dish. Add 2 thickly sliced medium eggplant and 1 minced garlic clove. Marinate at room temperature for 3 hours, stirring occasionally. Broil 6 inches from the heat source for 2 minutes on each side or until golden brown. The eggplant can also be grilled.

# SUMMER SUCCOTASH

### Lemon Dijon Sauce
2/3 cup mayonnaise
6 tablespoons buttermilk
4 teaspoons Dijon
  mustard
4 teaspoons fresh
  lemon juice
4 teaspoons sugar
1/2 teaspoon hot
  pepper sauce

### Succotash
2 large red bell peppers
Salt to taste
3 cups fresh or thawed
  frozen baby lima beans
5 cups fresh or thawed
  frozen corn kernels
2/3 cup thinly sliced
  green onions
Pepper to taste

*For the sauce*, whisk the mayonnaise, buttermilk, Dijon mustard, lemon juice, sugar and pepper sauce in a bowl until blended.

*For the succotash*, roast the bell peppers over a gas flame or broil until blackened on all sides. Place in a paper bag or bowl covered with plastic wrap and let stand for 10 minutes. Peel, seed and coarsely chop the bell peppers.

Cook the lima beans in salted water to cover in a large saucepan for 2 minutes or until done to taste; drain and cool. Combine with the peppers in a bowl. Add the corn and green onions.

Add enough of the sauce to coat well, tossing gently. Season with salt and pepper. Serve chilled or at room temperature.

NOTE: SUMMER SUCCOTASH CAN BE SERVED AS A SIDE DISH OR SALAD.

*Serves eight*

# SWEET POTATO CASSEROLE

**Pecan Topping**

- 1/2   cup packed light
       brown sugar
- 1/3   cup flour
- 3     tablespoons margarine
       or butter
- 1     cup chopped pecans

**Casserole**

- 3     cups hot mashed cooked
       sweet potatoes
- 1/2   cup sugar
- 2     large eggs
- 1/4   cup (1/2 stick)
       margarine or butter
- 1/2   cup milk
- 1/2   teaspoon vanilla extract
- 1/2   teaspoon salt

*For the topping,* combine the brown sugar, flour, margarine and pecans in a bowl and mix until crumbly.

*For the casserole,* combine the sweet potatoes, sugar, eggs, margarine, milk, vanilla and salt in a bowl and mix well. Spoon into a greased 1- to 1 1/2-quart baking dish.

Sprinkle the topping over the sweet potatoes. Bake at 350 degrees for 35 minutes.

NOTE: YOU MAY PREPARE THIS A DAY IN ADVANCE AND CHILL UNTIL TIME TO BAKE.

*Serves six*

## Cooking Tips

### VEGETABLE HINTS

To preserve the flavor of carrots, peas, beets, and corn, add a small amount of sugar to the water after cooking. Sand and dirt can be easily removed from fresh vegetables by soaking them in salted warm water for five minutes.

# LEMON ZUCCHINI

6 to 8 zucchini
Lemon juice to taste
3/4 cup seasoned
    bread crumbs
1/4 cup grated Parmesan
    cheese
6 tablespoons (3/4 stick)
    butter, melted
1/4 cup chopped parsley

Cut the zucchini into halves lengthwise and arrange cut side up in a buttered shallow baking dish. Drizzle with lemon juice.

Combine the bread crumbs, cheese and butter in a small bowl and mix well. Sprinkle over the zucchini. Bake at 350 degrees for 30 minutes. Sprinkle with the parsley.

*Serves twelve*

# ZUCCHINI AND FRESH THYME

1 garlic clove,
    thinly sliced
2 tablespoons olive oil
4 zucchini, sliced
1 teaspoon chopped
    fresh thyme
Salt and pepper to taste

Sauté the garlic in the olive oil in a sauté pan until tender. Add the zucchini, shaking the pan to coat with oil. Add the thyme, salt and pepper. Cook, covered, over low heat for 6 minutes or just until tender-crisp.

*Serves six*

# OVEN-ROASTED VEGETABLES

10 unpeeled whole small
    new potatoes
1 small onion
1 cup peeled baby carrots
1/4 cup olive oil
3 tablespoons lemon juice
3 garlic cloves, minced
1 tablespoon minced fresh
    rosemary or oregano
1 teaspoon salt
1/2 teaspoon pepper
1/2 small eggplant
1 medium red or green
    bell pepper

Cut the potatoes into quarters and the onion into wedges. Combine the potatoes, onion and carrots in a 9 × 13-inch roasting pan.

Mix the olive oil, lemon juice, garlic, rosemary, salt and pepper in a small bowl. Drizzle over the vegetables, tossing to coat well. Roast at 450 degrees for 30 minutes, stirring occasionally.

Cut the eggplant into quarters lengthwise and slice 1/2 inch thick. Cut the bell pepper into 1/2-inch strips. Add to the roasting pan and toss gently. Roast for 15 minutes longer.

*Serves eight*

# SUMMER RATATOUILLE

1 small globe eggplant
Salt for the eggplant
1 red onion, thinly sliced
1/4 cup olive oil
1 yellow or red bell
    pepper, cut into slices
2 garlic cloves, cut
    into halves
2 large tomatoes, sliced
1 teaspoon thyme
1 teaspoon oregano
1/4 cup vegetable stock
Salt and freshly ground
    pepper to taste
2 tablespoons chopped
    fresh parsley or basil

Cut the eggplant lengthwise into quarters. Cut each quarter into long, thin strips. Place in a colander and sprinkle with salt. Let stand for 30 minutes. Rinse under cold water. Pat dry with paper towels.

Sauté the onion in the olive oil in a large skillet over medium heat for 5 minutes or until tender. Stir in the bell pepper, garlic, tomatoes, thyme and oregano. Add the eggplant and stock. Simmer, covered, over low heat for 20 to 30 minutes or until tender, stirring occasionally.

Discard the garlic halves. Season with salt and pepper. Spoon into a serving dish. Sprinkle with the parsley.

*Serves four*

# ANTIPASTO RICE

1/2 cup tomato juice

1 1/2 cups water

1 cup uncooked rice

1 teaspoon dried
basil leaves

1 teaspoon dried
oregano leaves

1/2 teaspoon salt (optional)

1 (14-ounce) can
artichoke hearts,
drained, chopped

1 (7-ounce) jar roasted
red bell peppers,
drained, chopped

1 (2-ounce) can sliced
black olives, drained

2 tablespoons chopped
parsley

2 tablespoons lemon juice

1/2 teaspoon freshly
ground pepper

2 tablespoons grated
Parmesan cheese

Combine the tomato juice, water, rice, basil, oregano and salt in a 2- to 3-quart saucepan and bring to a boil, stirring once or twice. Reduce the heat and simmer, covered, for 15 minutes or until the rice is tender and the liquid is absorbed.

Add the artichokes, bell peppers, olives, parsley, lemon juice and pepper. Cook for 5 minutes or until heated through. Sprinkle with the cheese.

*Serves four*

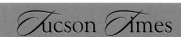

### SPRING TRAINING

Major league baseball comes to Tucson for spring training every March. Currently the Colorado Rockies, Chicago White Sox, and Arizona Diamondbacks all warm up for the season in the balmy Tucson climate.

# CILANTRO RISOTTO

6    cups chicken stock
1    small onion,
        thinly sliced
4    shallots, finely chopped
1    garlic clove, finely
        chopped
3    tablespoons olive oil
2    cups uncooked
        arborio rice
Kernels from 2 ears
        fresh corn
3    tablespoons grated
        Romano cheese
1 1/2 cups finely chopped,
        loosely packed
        fresh cilantro
1 1/2 teaspoons cumin
Salt and freshly ground
        pepper to taste

Bring the chicken stock to a simmer in a saucepan.

Sauté the onion, shallots and garlic in the heated olive oil in a large saucepan over medium heat for 3 minutes or until tender. Add the rice and sauté until coated well.

Add the heated chicken stock to the rice $1/2$ cup at a time and cook until the liquid is absorbed after each addition, stirring constantly; the entire cooking time will be about 20 to 25 minutes. Stir in the corn, cheese, cilantro, cumin, salt and pepper and cook just until heated through.

*Serves four*

# MANGO GINGER RICE

2   tablespoons thinly sliced
    green onions
2   garlic cloves, minced
1/3 cup chopped carrots
1   teaspoon grated
    gingerroot
2   teaspoons olive oil
1/2 cup chopped or thinly
    sliced fresh mango
2   tablespoons reduced-
    sodium soy sauce
3   tablespoons chicken
    broth or water
1   tablespoon cilantro
1 1/2 cups rice, cooked

Sauté the green onions, garlic, carrots and gingerroot lightly in the heated olive oil in a medium sauté pan. Add the mango, soy sauce, chicken broth and cilantro and cook for 2 minutes longer. Add the rice and mix well. Serve immediately or reheat with 2 tablespoons water in the microwave.

NOTE: COOK THE RICE FOR THIS DISH WITHOUT BUTTER OR SALT.

Serves six

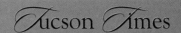

## MOUNTAIN RANGES

Four mountain ranges surround Tucson. The Santa Catalinas are to the north, the Santa Rita to the south, the Rincon Mountains to the east, and the Tucson Mountains to the west.

# Temptations from the Oven

## BREADS & BRUNCHES

## BRUNCH FOR FORE

*Visitors to Tucson spend more time and money on golf than
on any other form of recreation. The myriad of courses
available coupled with southern Arizona's mild winter weather
has made Tucson a golfer's haven. Whether it's fore
on the course or four at brunch, this meal is sure to score.*

## Menu

LEMON GINGER MUFFINS

SAVORY CHEESECAKE

SPINACH AND APPLE SALAD WITH BACON

BERRY SPARKLERS

ORANGE MARGARITAS

COFFEE AND TEA

# BLUEBERRY BUTTERMILK COFFEE CAKE

## Topping
- 2/3  cup sugar
- 1/2  cup chopped pecans
- 2  tablespoons butter, melted
- 1 1/2  teaspoons cinnamon
- 1/2  teaspoon nutmeg

## Coffee Cake
- 1  cup buttermilk
- 2  eggs
- 2  teaspoons vanilla extract
- 1 1/2  teaspoons packed orange zest
- 2  cups flour
- 1  cup sugar
- 1  tablespoon baking powder
- 1/4  teaspoon nutmeg
- 1/2  cup (1 stick) unsalted butter, chilled, cut into pieces
- 1 1/2  cups frozen unsweetened blueberries

*For the topping,* combine the sugar, pecans, butter, cinnamon and nutmeg in a bowl and mix well.

*For the coffee cake,* whisk the buttermilk, eggs, vanilla and orange zest in a small bowl. Combine the flour, sugar, baking powder and nutmeg in a large bowl and mix well. Cut in the butter until crumbly. Add the buttermilk mixture and mix well. Fold in the blueberries. Spoon into a buttered and floured 9 × 9-inch baking pan. Sprinkle with the topping.

Bake at 350 degrees for 1 hour and 5 minutes or until a wooden pick inserted in the center comes out clean. Cool on a wire rack.

*Serves sixteen*

# Quick Coffee Cake

2 cups flour
1 teaspoon baking powder
1 teaspoon baking soda
1/2 cup (1 stick) butter, softened
3/4 cup sugar
1 teaspoon vanilla extract
3 eggs
1 cup sour cream
1 (6-ounce) can almond paste or apricot jam
Confectioners' sugar

Sift the flour, baking powder and baking soda together. Cream the butter and sugar together in a mixing bowl until light and fluffy. Beat in the vanilla. Add the eggs 1 at a time, mixing well after each addition. Add the sifted dry ingredients alternately with the sour cream, mixing well after each addition.

Pour half of the batter into a greased 10-inch tube pan. Spread the almond paste over the batter, cutting with a knife to swirl. Pour the remaining batter over the paste.

Bake at 350 degrees for 50 minutes or until the cake springs back when touched lightly. Cool for 10 minutes in the pan. Invert onto a serving plate. Let stand until completely cooled. Sprinkle with confectioners' sugar.

*Serves sixteen to twenty*

## Tucson Times

### Old Tucson

Tucson is one of the oldest continually inhabited settlements in the United States. The first country to lay claim on the Tucson area was Spain, followed by Mexico. Finally in 1854 the Gadsden Purchase brought Tucson into the United States. In 1856, American troops showed up to take possession of the desert village.

# DANISH PASTRY

### Crust

$^1/2$ cup (1 stick) cold
 butter
1 cup flour
2 tablespoons cold water

### Filling

1 cup water
$^1/2$ cup (1 stick) butter
1 teaspoon almond
 extract
1 cup flour
3 eggs

### Frosting

2 tablespoons butter,
 softened
$1^1/2$ teaspoons vanilla
 extract
$1^1/2$ cups confectioners'
 sugar
1 to 2 tablespoons water
$^1/4$ cup sliced almonds

*For the crust*, cut the butter into the flour in a bowl until crumbly. Add the water, mixing with a fork until mixture forms a ball. Shape into a $^1/2$-inch thick rectangle on a baking sheet.

*For the filling*, combine the water, butter and almond extract in a saucepan. Bring to a boil. Add the flour quickly, stirring to prevent lumps. Add the eggs 1 at a time, mixing well after each addition. Spread evenly over the pastry. Bake at 350 degrees for 1 hour or until golden brown. Let stand until cooled.

*For the frosting*, combine the butter, vanilla, confectioners' sugar and enough water to make of a spreading consistency in a bowl and mix well. Spread over the baked pastry. Sprinkle with the sliced almonds.

*Serves ten to twelve*

# JALAPEÑO JACK CORN BREAD

2¹/₂ cups cornmeal
2¹/₂ cups flour
¹/₄ cup sugar
1 tablespoon salt
2 tablespoons baking
   powder
4 eggs
¹/₂ cup vegetable oil
2 cups milk
¹/₂ cup chopped red
   bell pepper
¹/₄ cup chopped jalapeño
   chiles or diced
   green chiles
2 cups shredded
   Monterey Jack cheese

Combine the cornmeal, flour, sugar, salt and baking powder in a bowl and mix well. Combine the eggs and oil in a separate bowl and mix well. Add to the dry ingredients and mix well.

Add the milk, bell pepper, chiles and cheese and mix just until blended. Spoon into a greased 9 × 13-inch baking pan. Bake at 375 degrees for 20 minutes.

*Serves twelve*

## Beverage Tips

### SERVING WINE

Serve appetizer wines at room temperature or chilled to about 50 degrees. White wines should also be chilled to about 50 degrees to serve. Red dinner wines should be served at 65 degrees. If the room temperature is above 65 degrees, refrigerate red wine for 15 minutes before serving.

# APPLE FRENCH TOAST

1 large loaf French bread
8 extra-large eggs
3$^1$/2 cups 2% milk
$^1$/2 cup sugar
1 tablespoon vanilla
  extract
6 to 8 medium cooking
  apples such as
  McIntosh and Cortland
$^1$/2 cup sugar
1 tablespoon cinnamon
1 teaspoon nutmeg
1 tablespoon butter

Cut the bread into $^1$/2-inch-thick slices. Arrange tightly in a single layer in a 9 × 13-inch baking pan sprayed with nonstick cooking spray.

Combine the eggs, milk, $^1$/2 cup sugar and vanilla in a bowl and whisk for 30 seconds. Pour half of the mixture over the bread slices.

Peel and slice the apples. Arrange the apple slices over the bread, covering it completely. Pour the remaining egg mixture over the layers.

Combine $^1$/2 cup sugar, cinnamon and nutmeg in a small bowl. Sprinkle over the apples. Dot with the butter. Refrigerate, covered, for 8 hours or longer.

Bake at 350 degrees for 1 hour. Let stand for 10 minutes. Serve with warm syrup and confectioners' sugar.

*Serves six*

# ORANGE FRENCH TOAST

1    loaf French bread,
      cut into 1-inch thick
      slices or 1 loaf Texas
      Toast bread
4    eggs
2/3  cup freshly squeezed
      orange juice
1/2  cup milk
1/4  cup sugar
1/2  teaspoon vanilla extract
1/4  teaspoon freshly grated
      nutmeg
1/2  cup pecans, chopped
      (optional)
1    teaspoon grated
      orange zest
1/3  cup butter, melted
Confectioners' sugar

Arrange the bread slices tightly in a single layer in a 9 × 13-inch baking pan sprayed with nonstick cooking spray.

Whisk the eggs, orange juice, milk, sugar, vanilla and nutmeg in a bowl. Pour over the bread slices. Sprinkle with the pecans and orange zest. Chill, covered, for 8 to 12 hours.

Pour the melted butter over the top. Bake at 400 degrees for 20 to 25 minutes or until golden brown. Sprinkle with confectioners' sugar. Serve with syrup and fresh fruit.

*Serves four to six*

## Other Temptations

### BROWN SUGAR SYRUP

Mix 1 cup heavy cream and 1 cup packed brown sugar in a saucepan. Cook over medium-low heat until the brown sugar dissolves, stirring constantly; do not boil. Stir in 1 teaspoon butter and 1 teaspoon vanilla extract. Cook just until the butter melts.

# APPLE NUT MUFFINS

2   eggs
1/2  cup sour cream
1/4  cup (1/2 stick) butter,
     melted
1 1/2 cups peeled, grated
     Granny Smith apples
2   cups flour
2   teaspoons baking
     powder
1/2  teaspoon baking soda
1/4  teaspoon salt
3/4  teaspoon cardamom
2/3  cup sugar
1/2  cup toasted chopped
     walnuts
1/2  cup sugar
1/4  cup toasted chopped
     walnuts
1   teaspoon allspice

Whisk the eggs, sour cream, butter and apples in a bowl.

Sift the flour, baking powder, baking soda, salt, cardamom and 2/3 cup sugar together. Stir into the egg mixture just until blended. Stir in 1/2 cup walnuts. Pour into 12 greased muffin cups.

Combine 1/2 cup sugar, 1/4 cup walnuts and allspice in a bowl and mix well. Sprinkle over the batter.

Bake at 375 degrees for 22 minutes or until muffins spring back when lightly pressed. Cool on a wire rack.

*Serves twelve*

## Cooking Tips

### REDUCE FAT

Muffins, brownies, and carrot cake can be converted to delicious lower-fat versions by substituting a fruit preserve for the oil or butter in the recipe.

# LEMON GINGER MUFFINS

Zest of 2 lemons
2/3 cup sugar
1 1/2 tablespoons minced
    gingerroot
2/3 cup orange juice
1/4 cup plain nonfat yogurt
1 egg white
3 tablespoons canola oil
1 teaspoon vanilla extract
2 cups flour
2 teaspoons baking
    powder
1/2 teaspoon baking soda
1/8 teaspoon salt

Process the lemon zest and sugar in a food processor for 1 minute or until well mixed and sugar appears yellow, reserving 2 tablespoons of the mixture. Add the gingerroot to the remaining mixture in the food processor and mix well. Add the orange juice, yogurt, egg white, canola oil and vanilla and mix well.

Combine the flour, baking powder, baking soda and salt in a large bowl and mix well. Add the orange juice mixture, stirring just until moistened. Fill 12 greased muffin cups 2/3 full. Sprinkle with the reserved lemon zest mixture.

Bake at 400 degrees for 15 minutes or until light brown and tops spring back when lightly touched. Cool in the pan for 5 minutes.

Serves twelve

# WHEAT GERM MUFFINS

1/3  cup butter, melted
1/3  cup honey
2    eggs
1/2  teaspoon almond
     extract
1    teaspoon vanilla extract
1/2  cup nonfat dry milk
     powder
1    cup wheat germ
3/4  teaspoon baking powder
1/4  teaspoon salt
1/2  cup slivered almonds or
     sunflower kernels
1/2  cup raisins
1/2  cup shredded coconut
     (optional)

Combine the butter, honey, eggs, almond extract and vanilla in a bowl and mix well. Add the nonfat dry milk powder, wheat germ, baking powder and salt and mix well. Stir in the almonds, raisins and coconut.

Fill 12 paper-lined muffin cups 2/3 full. Bake at 350 degrees for 25 minutes.

Serves twelve

## Other Temptations

### DILL POPOVERS

Heat a 12-cup muffin pan or 6-cup popover pan in a 450-degree oven. Beat 1 cup milk with 1 tablespoon melted butter in a bowl. Beat in a sifted mixture of 1 cup flour and a pinch of salt. Beat in 2 eggs and stir in 1/4 cup minced fresh dill. Grease the heated popover cups with 1 tablespoon butter and sprinkle with 2 tablespoons flour. Spoon in the batter and bake at 450 degrees for 15 minutes. Reduce the temperature to 375 degrees and bake for 10 to 15 minutes longer or until crisp and brown.

# LEMON YOGURT PANCAKES

1 egg
1/2 cup lemon yogurt
1/2 cup milk
1 tablespoon sugar
1/2 teaspoon grated
   lemon zest
1/8 teaspoon nutmeg
1 cup flour
1 teaspoon baking powder
1/2 teaspoon baking soda

Whisk the egg, yogurt, milk, sugar, lemon zest, nutmeg, flour, baking powder and baking soda in a bowl. Pour 1/4 cup at a time onto a lightly greased hot griddle. Cook until golden brown on both sides.

*Serves eight*

# PUMPKIN CLOVE PANCAKES

2 cups flour
6 tablespoons brown
   sugar
1 1/2 teaspoons baking
   powder
1/2 teaspoon baking soda
1/2 teaspoon ground cloves
1/2 teaspoon salt
1 2/3 cups buttermilk
3/4 cup canned solid-pack
   pumpkin
3 eggs
2 tablespoons butter,
   melted

Combine the flour, brown sugar, baking powder, baking soda, cloves and salt in a bowl and mix well.

Whisk the buttermilk, pumpkin, eggs and butter in a separate bowl. Whisk into the dry ingredients until smooth. Pour 1/4 cup at a time onto a lightly greased hot griddle.

Cook until golden brown on both sides. Serve with maple syrup.

*Serves sixteen*

# SOUR CREAM ORANGE ROLLS

1    *envelope dry yeast*
$1/2$    *cup warm water*
$1/4$    *cup sugar*
1    *teaspoon salt*
2    *eggs*
$1/2$    *cup sour cream*
6    *tablespoons butter, melted*
$3^1/2$ *cups flour*
2    *tablespoons butter, melted*
$1^1/2$ *cups sugar*
4    *tablespoons grated orange zest*
$3/4$    *cup sugar*
$1/2$    *cup sour cream*
2    *tablespoons grated orange zest*
$1/2$    *cup (1 stick) butter, softened*

Dissolve the yeast in the warm water in a large mixing bowl. Beat in the sugar, salt, eggs, $1/2$ cup sour cream, and 6 tablespoons butter. Beat in 2 cups of the flour gradually. Knead in the remaining $1^1/2$ cups flour until smooth and elastic. Place in a greased bowl, turning to coat the surface. Let rise, covered, in a warm place for 2 hours or until doubled in bulk. Knead on a floured surface 15 times. Divide the dough into 2 portions.

Roll one portion into a 12-inch circle. Brush with 1 tablespoon of the butter. Sprinkle with $3/4$ cup of the sugar and 2 tablespoons of the orange zest. Cut into 12 wedges. Roll wedges up from the wide end. Shape into crescents. Place, point-side down, on a greased baking sheet. Repeat with the remaining portion of dough. Cover with waxed paper. Let rise until doubled in bulk.

Bake at 350 degrees for 20 minutes. Cool slightly on a wire rack. Combine $3/4$ cup sugar, $1/2$ cup sour cream, 2 tablespoons orange zest and $1/2$ cup butter in a saucepan. Bring to a boil. Boil for 3 minutes, stirring constantly. Cool slightly and drizzle over the crescents.

*Serves twenty-four*

# CRANBERRY DATE SCONES

3 cups flour
1/2 cup sugar
Zest of 1 large orange
1 tablespoon baking
powder
1/2 teaspoon baking soda
1/2 teaspoon salt
3/4 cup (1 1/2 sticks)
unsalted butter
1 cup cranberries
1/2 cup chopped
pitted dates
1 cup cold buttermilk
2 tablespoons sugar
1/8 teaspoon cinnamon
Allspice to taste
Mace to taste

Line a 12 × 15-inch baking sheet with parchment paper.

Combine the flour, 1/2 cup sugar, orange zest, baking powder, baking soda and salt in a bowl and mix well. Cut in the butter until crumbly. Add the cranberries and dates and toss to combine. Stir in the buttermilk, forming a stiff dough. Knead gently on a lightly floured surface just until dough holds together. Divide the dough into 2 portions. Shape each portion into a 3/4-inch-thick 7-inch round.

Combine 2 tablespoons sugar, cinnamon, allspice and mace in a small bowl and mix well. Sprinkle over the circles. Cut each round into 6 wedges. Place the wedges 1/2 inch apart on the prepared baking sheet.

Bake at 400 degrees for 20 to 25 minutes or until golden brown. Serve warm.

*Serves twelve*

## Cooking Tips

### CRANBERRIES

Cranberries are one of only three major fruits native to North America. The other two are blueberries and Concord grapes. The Pilgrims called cranberries crane berries, possibly because of the crane's fondness for the red berries. Some people call them bounceberries because they bounce when ripe. The peak season for cranberries is from October through December, making them a favorite for the holiday season. Look for bright red berries that are firm and glossy.

# BUTTERMILK SCONES

1 cup flour
$1/2$ teaspoon baking soda
$1/4$ teaspoon salt
3 tablespoons butter, chilled
$1/2$ cup buttermilk

Combine the flour, baking soda and salt in a bowl and mix well. Cut in the butter until crumbly. Stir in the buttermilk. Roll the dough to $1/2$-inch thickness on a lightly floured surface. Cut into 2-inch rounds. Place on a baking sheet. Bake at 400 degrees for 10 to 15 minutes.

*Serves twelve*

# GINGER SCONES

6 cups cake flour
$1/2$ cup sugar
3 tablespoons baking powder
$3^1/4$ cups ($6^1/2$ sticks) butter, cut into $1/2$-inch pieces
$1^1/2$ cups crystallized gingerroot
3 cups heavy cream

Combine the flour, sugar and baking powder in a bowl and mix well. Cut in the butter until crumbly. Add the gingerroot and $2^1/2$ cups of the cream and mix well; do not overmix.

Pat the dough to $3/4$-inch thickness on a lightly floured surface. Cut with a biscuit cutter. Place on a baking sheet. Freeze for 15 to 20 minutes. Brush the tops with the remaining $1/2$ cup cream. Bake at 350 degrees for 30 minutes.

*Serves seventy-two*

# POPPY SEED BREAD

### Bread
| | |
|---|---|
| 3 | eggs |
| 1¹/2 | cups milk |
| 1 | cup plus 2 tablespoons vegetable oil |
| 1¹/2 | teaspoons almond extract |
| 1¹/2 | teaspoons vanilla extract |
| 1¹/2 | teaspoons butter flavoring |
| 3 | cups flour |
| 1¹/2 | teaspoons salt |
| 1¹/2 | teaspoons baking powder |
| 2¹/4 | cups sugar |
| 2 | tablespoons poppy seeds |

### Glaze
| | |
|---|---|
| ¹/4 | cup orange juice |
| ¹/2 | teaspoon almond extract |
| ¹/2 | teaspoon vanilla extract |
| ¹/2 | teaspoon butter flavoring |
| ³/4 | cup confectioners' sugar |

*For the bread,* combine the eggs, milk, oil, almond extract, vanilla and butter flavoring in a bowl and mix well. Combine the flour, salt, baking powder, sugar and poppy seeds in a separate bowl and mix well. Add the egg mixture and mix well. Pour into three 5 × 9-inch greased loaf pans. Bake at 350 degrees for 1 hour. Cool in the pans for 10 minutes. Remove to a wire rack to cool completely.

*For the glaze,* combine the orange juice, almond extract, vanilla, butter flavoring and confectioners' sugar in a bowl and mix well. Poke holes in the top of the cooled loaves. Brush the glaze over the loaves.

*Serves thirty*

## Tucson Times

### ARIZONA NAMES
Arizona nicknames include "The Grand Canyon State," "The Copper State," and "The Valentine State" because it became the 48th state on February 14, 1912. The name Tucson is derived from the Pima word Stjukshone, roughly meaning spring, for the spring at the foot of Sentinel Peak.

# SPICED BROWN SUGAR CARROT BREAD

3    cups unbleached flour
2    teaspoons cinnamon
1<sup>1</sup>/2 teaspoons baking
      powder
1<sup>1</sup>/2 teaspoons baking soda
1    teaspoon crushed
      cardamom seeds
<sup>1</sup>/2   teaspoon salt
4    eggs
1<sup>1</sup>/2 cups packed brown
      sugar
<sup>1</sup>/2   cup sugar
1    cup canola oil
1    teaspoon vanilla extract
Zest of 1 lemon
2<sup>1</sup>/2 cups shredded carrots

Combine the flour, cinnamon, baking powder, baking soda, cardamom and salt in a bowl and mix well.

Beat the eggs, brown sugar and sugar in a mixing bowl until smooth. Add the canola oil in a thin stream, beating at high speed for 2 minutes or until doubled in volume. Beat in the vanilla and lemon zest. Fold in the carrots. Beat in the dry ingredients at low speed in 3 batches, beating well after each addition. Pour the batter into 2 greased and floured 4 × 8-inch loaf pans.

Bake at 350 degrees for 50 to 60 minutes or until a wooden pick inserted in the center comes out clean. Cool in the pans for 10 minutes. Remove to a wire rack to cool completely.

NOTE: YOU MAY WRAP THE COOLED LOAVES TIGHTLY IN PLASTIC WRAP AND FREEZE FOR UP TO 2 MONTHS.

Serves twenty

# CURRIED EGGS AND MUSHROOMS

5    hard-cooked eggs
8    ounces mushrooms
2    tablespoons butter
2    tablespoons flour
1    cup half-and-half
1/4  teaspoon salt
1/8  teaspoon paprika
1    teaspoon sherry
1/4  cup shredded
      sharp cheese
1/2  teaspoon curry powder
1    tablespoon chili sauce
Dry bread crumbs
Butter

Peel the eggs and cut into quarters. Sauté the mushrooms in a nonstick skillet until tender. Heat 2 tablespoons butter in a separate skillet until melted. Stir in the flour and cook for 5 to 10 minutes or until light brown. Whisk in the half-and-half gradually. Stir in the salt, paprika and sherry. Cook until the sauce is smooth, stirring constantly.

Stir in the cheese, curry powder and chili sauce. Stir in the eggs and mushrooms. Spoon into an 8 × 8-inch baking dish. Sprinkle the bread crumbs over the egg mixture. Dot with butter.

Bake at 350 degrees for 30 to 40 minutes or until hot and bubbly.

*Serves four*

## Beverage Tips

### BERRY SPARKLERS

Spoon 3 tablespoons of puréed strawberries into each tulip champagne glass. Fill the glasses with chilled Champagne or sparkling wine and garnish with a whole strawberry and a sprig of fresh mint.

# SUMMERTIME FRITTATA

1 pound thin-skinned
  potatoes, chopped
1 pound mushrooms,
  sliced
2 teaspoons olive oil
1/4 cup water
6 to 8 green onions, sliced
8 eggs
2/3 cup shredded cheese
1/2 cup water
Salt and pepper to taste

Combine the potatoes, mushrooms, olive oil and 1/4 cup water in a 12-inch ovenproof skillet. Cook, covered, over medium-high heat for 12 minutes or until the potatoes are tender, stirring occasionally. Remove the cover. Cook until the liquid evaporates.

Reserve 2 tablespoons of the green onions. Combine the remaining green onions, eggs, cheese and 1/2 cup water in a bowl and mix well. Pour over the potato mixture in the skillet.

Cook over low heat for 4 minutes or until mixture begins to set around the edge. Broil 6 inches from the heat source until the frittata is set. Season with salt and pepper. Sprinkle with the reserved green onions. Serve with salsa.

*Serves eight*

## Beverage Tips

### ORANGE BANANA SHAKE

Combine 2 cups low-fat vanilla ice cream or yogurt, 1 1/2 cups orange juice, one 6-ounce can pineapple juice and 1 chopped medium banana in a blender and process until smooth. Garnish with fresh fruit if desired and serve immediately for a brunch or snack treat.

# HAM AND EGG BISCUIT PIZZAS

**Biscuit Pizza Crusts**

2 cups flour
2 teaspoons baking
   powder
1 teaspoon salt
1/2 cup (1 stick) butter,
   chilled, chopped
1/2 cup plus 2 tablespoons
   milk

**Filling**

2 cups shredded
   Muenster or Monterey
   Jack cheese
3 red, green or yellow
   bell peppers, cut
   into strips
1 onion, thinly sliced
1 1/2 tablespoons unsalted
   butter
1 cup finely chopped
   cooked ham
6 large eggs
Watercress sprigs

*For the crusts*, whisk the flour, baking powder and salt in a bowl. Cut in the butter until the mixture is the consistency of coarse meal. Add the milk and mix just until the mixture forms a ball.

Knead the dough gently on a floured surface 6 times and divide into 6 portions. Shape each portion into a 7-inch circle. Pinch up about 1 inch around the edges to form a rim. Place on a buttered large baking sheet.

*For the filling*, sprinkle the cheese evenly in the biscuit shells. Cook the bell peppers and onion in the butter in a large heavy skillet over medium heat until tender, stirring frequently. Stir in the ham. Spoon into the prepared shells, making a well in the center of each.

Break 1 egg carefully into each well. Bake the pizzas in the center of a 425-degree oven for 12 to 15 minutes or just until the egg yolks are set. Top with watercress and serve immediately.

*Serves six*

# SAVORY CHEESECAKE

$1^1/3$ cups toasted
   bread crumbs
5   tablespoons butter,
   melted
24  ounces cream cheese,
   softened
$1/4$  cup heavy cream
$1/2$  teaspoon salt
$1/2$  teaspoon dry mustard
$1/4$  teaspoon nutmeg
$1/4$  teaspoon cayenne
   pepper
1   cup shredded
   Gruyère cheese
4   eggs
1   (10-ounce) package
   frozen chopped spinach,
   thawed
$2^1/2$ tablespoons chopped
   green onions
8   ounces mushrooms,
   finely chopped
3   tablespoons butter
Salt and pepper to taste

Combine the bread crumbs and 5 tablespoons butter in a bowl and mix well. Press over the bottom and up the side of a buttered 9-inch springform pan. Bake at 350 degrees for 8 minutes.

Beat the cream cheese, cream, $1/2$ teaspoon salt, mustard, nutmeg and cayenne pepper in a mixing bowl until smooth.

Combine the Gruyère cheese and eggs in a bowl and mix well. Add half of the cream cheese mixture and mix well.

Press the spinach to remove excess moisture. Add the spinach and green onions to the remaining cream cheese mixture.

Sauté the mushrooms in 3 tablespoons butter in a skillet until tender.

Layer the spinach mixture, sautéed mushrooms and Gruyère mixture in the prepared crust. Season with salt and pepper to taste.

Bake at 325 degrees for $1^1/4$ hours. Turn off the oven, leaving the cheesecake in the oven with the door ajar for 1 hour. Remove to a wire rack. Cool to room temperature. Serve with warm marinara sauce.

*Serves twelve*

# OLD TUCSON STUDIOS

*Old Tucson Studios came to life in 1939, when Columbia Pictures selected a Pima County-owned
site on which to build a replica of 1860s Tucson for the movie Arizona. The film, which
starred William Holden and Jean Arthur, set a new standard for realism in westerns, initiating the
move away from studio backdrops to outdoor settings. Since then, Old Tucson has hosted productions
and stars of such movies as Rio Bravo in 1959, Hombre in 1966, The Three Amigos in 1986,
Tombstone in 1993, and television's "Little House on the Prairie" from 1977 to 1983.
Old Tucson Studios has played a prominent role in shaping the world's perception of the Old West,
and rightfully claims the title of "Hollywood in the Desert."*

# Bacon and Fromage Quiche

**Crust**

1¹/3 cups flour
1/8  teaspoon salt
1/2  cup (1 stick) butter,
     chilled, cut into
     small pieces
2 to 3 tablespoons cold
     water

**Filling**

4    eggs
1¹/2 cups light cream
1/4  teaspoon dried thyme
1/8  teaspoon white pepper
10   slices lean bacon, crisp-
     cooked, crumbled
1/2  cup shredded
     Gruyère cheese
1/2  cup shredded white
     Cheddar cheese

*For the crust,* combine the flour and salt in a large bowl and mix well. Cut in the butter until crumbly. Add the water 1 tablespoon at a time, mixing with a fork until the mixture forms a ball. Chill, covered with plastic wrap, for 30 minutes or longer.

Roll into an 11-inch circle on a lightly floured surface. Fit into a 9-inch pie plate. Trim the edge, leaving a 1/4-inch overhang. Fold under, forming an edge 1/4 inch high. Prick the dough several times with a fork. Line with foil and fill with pie weights or dried beans.

Bake at 375 degrees for 10 minutes. Remove the foil and weights. Bake for 5 minutes longer or until golden brown. Remove to a wire rack to cool.

*For the filling,* whisk the eggs, cream, thyme and pepper in a bowl. Pour into the piecrust. Sprinkle the bacon, Gruyère cheese and Cheddar cheese over the egg mixture. Bake for 30 minutes or until golden and set. Serve warm.

*Serves eight*

# BACON AND MUSHROOM QUICHE

1   unbaked (9-inch)
    pie shell
6   slices bacon
1   small onion, minced
6   ounces fresh white
    mushrooms,
    thinly sliced
Salt and pepper to taste
3   eggs
3/4 cup milk
1/2 cup shredded sharp
    Cheddar cheese

Prick the pie shell several times with a fork. Bake at 400 degrees for 10 to 12 minutes or until golden brown. Remove to a wire rack. Reduce the oven temperature to 375 degrees.

Cook the bacon in a skillet until crisp. Set the bacon on paper towels to drain. Pour off the drippings, reserving 1 tablespoon in the skillet. Cook the onion in the drippings until tender. Add the mushrooms and cook until tender. Drain off all liquids. Crumble the bacon and stir into the mushroom mixture. Season with salt and pepper. Whisk the eggs and milk in a large bowl. Stir in the mushroom mixture and the cheese. Pour into the prepared piecrust. Set the pie plate on a baking sheet.

Bake for 35 minutes or until golden brown. Let stand for 10 minutes.

*Serves six*

## Tucson Times

### SEEING STARS

There are more observatories within a 50-mile radius of Tucson than in any other area of comparable size in the world. Flandrau Planetarium on the campus of the University of Arizona has hands-on displays and an IMAX presentation, and visitors can look for planets and stars on clear nights Wednesdays through Saturdays with no admission charge.

# New Mexican Quiche

8  ounces bulk hot Italian
   sausage
6  corn tortillas
8  ounces Monterey Jack
   cheese, shredded
8  ounces refried beans
2  tablespoons diced green
   chiles
2  eggs
2  cups half-and-half
$1/2$  teaspoon salt

Brown the sausage in a skillet, stirring until crumbly; drain. Line a 9-inch pie plate with the tortillas, leaving a $1/2$-inch overhang. Sprinkle half of the cheese over the tortillas. Layer the sausage, beans and chiles over the cheese. Beat the eggs in a medium bowl. Add the half-and-half and salt and mix well. Pour over the layers. Sprinkle the remaining cheese over the top.

Bake at 325 degrees for 35 minutes or until set in the center. Serve warm.

*Serves six*

# Spinach and Feta Quiche

1  (10-ounce) package
   frozen chopped spinach,
   thawed
6  ounces feta cheese,
   crumbled
$1/2$  cup cottage cheese
6  green onions, sliced
1  tablespoon olive oil
1  teaspoon dried basil
$1/2$  teaspoon pepper
$1/4$  teaspoon garlic salt
4  eggs
$1/2$  cup milk
1  unbaked (9-inch)
   pie shell

Press the spinach to remove excess moisture. Process the feta cheese, cottage cheese, green onions, olive oil, basil, pepper and garlic salt in a food processor until smooth. Add the eggs and milk and mix well. Add the spinach and process briefly. Pour into the pie shell.

Bake at 400 degrees for 20 minutes. Reduce the oven temperature to 350 degrees. Bake for 15 to 20 minutes longer or until a knife inserted in the center comes out clean. Cool on a wire rack for 10 minutes. Serve warm or at room temperature.

*Serves six*

# BREAKFAST TOSTADA

1 tablespoon margarine
1 flour tortilla
2 eggs
1/3 cup milk
1/3 cup shredded Monterey Jack or Cheddar cheese
1 tablespoon chopped green onions
1/8 teaspoon cilantro (optional)
1/8 teaspoon dry mustard
1/8 teaspoon chile powder
1/8 teaspoon salt
1 tablespoon chopped green chiles

Heat the margarine in a skillet until melted. Add the tortilla. Cook until hot and softened, turning once. Fit into a 2-cup ovenproof bowl.

Combine the eggs and milk in a separate bowl and mix well. Add the cheese, green onions, cilantro, mustard, chile powder, salt and chiles and mix well. Spoon into the tortilla. Bake at 350 degrees for 30 minutes.

*Serves one*

## Other Temptations

### THREE-CHEESE CASSEROLE

Combine 6 beaten eggs, 1 cup milk, 4 cups shredded Monterey Jack cheese, 3 ounces cubed cream cheese, 2 cups cottage cheese, 1/2 cup flour, 1 teaspoon baking powder, 1 1/2 teaspoons sugar and 1/2 teaspoon salt in a mixing bowl and mix well. Spoon into a baking dish and drizzle with 1/2 cup melted butter. Bake at 375 degrees for 45 minutes or until set.

# Sweet Temptations

## DESSERTS

# MONSOON TEA PARTY

*The monsoons are a welcomed respite that signal the beginning
of the end of summer. When the conditions are right in July
and August, dark clouds well up from the south and roll in by late
afternoon, bringing amazing electrical storms and cloudbursts
that flood the streets and cool the air. While inside, pamper yourself
and friends with a tea party complete with these delicacies.*

## Menu

CRANBERRY DATE SCONES

GINGER SCONES

AVOCADO AND MOZZARELLA SALAD

HUMMUS WITH PITA WEDGES
AND CRUDITÉS

CHOCOLATE DECADENCE

ASSORTED TEAS

# APPLE CRUMBLE

4 to 5 medium Pippin,
    Jonathan or Winesap
    apples
1/3  cup orange juice
1/4  cup sugar
1/2  cup packed
    brown sugar
3/4  teaspoon cinnamon
1/4  teaspoon salt
3/4  cup flour
1/4  cup (1/2 stick) butter

Peel and cut the apples into slices. Arrange evenly in a buttered 9 × 13-inch baking dish. Combine the orange juice and sugar in a small bowl and mix well. Pour over the apples. Combine the brown sugar, cinnamon, salt and flour in a bowl and mix well. Cut in the butter until crumbly. Sprinkle evenly over the apples. Bake at 375 degrees for 40 minutes or until the topping is brown and the apples are tender. Serve warm with custard sauce, cream or ice cream.

*Serves six*

# BLUEBERRY, PEACH AND CHERRY COBBLER

1/2  cup sugar
1    tablespoon cornstarch
4    cups blueberries, cut-up
    peaches and cherries
2    tablespoons water
1    cup baking mix
1/4  cup milk
1    tablespoon sugar
1    tablespoon butter,
    softened

Combine 1/2 cup sugar and cornstarch in a saucepan and mix well. Stir in the fruit and water. Bring to a boil, stirring constantly. Boil for 1 minute, stirring constantly. Pour into a 11/2-quart baking dish. Combine the baking mix, milk, 1 tablespoon sugar and butter in a bowl and mix until a soft dough forms. Drop by tablespoonfuls onto the hot fruit mixture. Bake at 350 degrees for 15 to 20 minutes or until golden brown.

*Serves six*

# SOUTHERN CHERRY CRUMBLE

**Crust**

1    *cup flour*
1/2  *teaspoon salt*
1/3  *cup shortening, chilled*
1/4  *cup ice water*

**Filling**

5    *cups pitted sweet or*
      *sour cherries*
2/3  *cup sugar for sweet*
      *cherries, or 1 1/3 cups*
      *sugar for sour cherries*
3    *tablespoons cornstarch*
1/4  *teaspoon salt*

**Topping**

3/4  *cup packed dark*
      *brown sugar*
3/4  *cup flour*
1/2  *teaspoon nutmeg*
1/3  *cup butter, chilled, cut*
      *into small pieces*

*For the crust,* combine the flour and salt in a bowl. Cut in the shortening until crumbly. Add the water 1 tablespoon at a time, mixing with a fork until the mixture forms a ball. Chill, covered with plastic wrap, for 30 minutes. Roll into a 12-inch circle on a floured surface. Fit into a 9-inch pie plate. Trim the excess dough, leaving a 1-inch overhang. Make a decorative edge.

*For the filling,* combine the cherries, sugar, cornstarch and salt in a bowl and mix well. Spoon into the pastry-lined pie plate.

*For the topping,* combine the brown sugar, flour and nutmeg in a bowl and mix well. Cut in the butter until crumbly. Sprinkle evenly over the cherry mixture.

Bake on the bottom rack of a 400-degree oven for 35 minutes or until the topping is light brown and filling is bubbly, covering with foil if the topping or crust brown too quickly. Place on a wire rack to cool.

*Serves eight*

## Tucson Times

### TUCSON'S WATER

Tucson's two main rivers—the Rillito, or little creek, and the Santa Cruz—have water only after heavy rains during the summer monsoons or winter rains. The soil in Tucson is composed of sand, clay, and rock, none of which have great absorption qualities, thus the water from the rains travels through arroyos, or dry washes, into the rivers.

# LEMON ICE

1 teaspoon unflavored
  gelatin
1 tablespoon cold water
4 cups boiling water
4 cups sugar
1/4 teaspoon salt
1 cup lemon juice
4 egg whites

Soften the gelatin in the cold water in a bowl for
5 minutes. Combine the boiling water and sugar in a
mixing bowl and stir until the sugar dissolves. Add the
salt, lemon juice and gelatin mixture, stirring until the
gelatin dissolves. Place in the freezer until partially frozen.
Beat at medium speed until smooth. Return to the freezer.
Freeze until partially frozen. Beat at medium speed until
smooth. Beat the egg whites in a separate bowl until stiff
peaks form. Fold into the lemon mixture. Freeze, covered,
until ready to serve, stirring occasionally.

Serves eight

# CHOCOLATE RASPBERRY FONDUE

2 medium bananas
2 medium kiwifruit
2 small pears
2 cups strawberries
2 small oranges
12 ounces milk chocolate,
   broken into small pieces
1/4 cup milk
1/4 cup raspberry liqueur

Cut the bananas into bite-size pieces. Peel the kiwifruit
and cut each into 8 wedges. Cut each pear into 8 wedges.
Hull the strawberries. Peel and section the oranges.
Arrange decoratively on a serving platter.

Heat the chocolate in a double boiler over hot, but not
boiling, water until the chocolate is melted smooth,
stirring frequently. Whisk in the milk and liqueur. Cook
for 2 to 3 minutes longer or until the mixture is heated
through, stirring frequently. Pour into a small fondue pot.
Keep warm over low heat. Spear the fruit pieces using
fondue forks and dip into the warm chocolate mixture.

Serves eight

# CHOCOLATE CHEESECAKE

**Crust**

1 1/2 cups finely crushed
    chocolate wafers
1/3  cup margarine, melted

**Filling**

8   ounces cream cheese,
    softened
1/4  cup sugar
1   teaspoon vanilla extract
2   egg yolks, beaten
1   cup chocolate chips,
    melted
2   egg whites
1/4  cup sugar
1   cup whipping cream,
    whipped
3/4  cup chopped pecans

*For the crust,* combine the chocolate wafers and the margarine in a bowl and mix well. Press over the bottom and up the side of a 9-inch springform pan. Bake at 325 degrees for 10 minutes.

*For the filling,* combine the cream cheese, 1/4 cup sugar and vanilla in a bowl and mix well. Stir in a mixture of the egg yolks and melted chocolate chips. Beat the egg whites in a mixing bowl until soft peaks form. Beat in 1/4 cup sugar until the soft peaks hold their shape. Fold into the chocolate mixture. Fold in the whipped cream. Pour into the prepared crust. Sprinkle the pecans over the top. Freeze until firm. To serve the cheesecake, thaw to room temperature.

*Serves eight to ten*

## Other Temptations

### PEANUT BUTTER CHOCOLATE FONDUE

Combine 6 ounces of semisweet chocolate, 1/2 cup sugar and 1/2 cup milk in a saucepan. Cook over low heat until the chocolate melts, stirring to blend. Stir in 1/2 cup chunky peanut butter. Serve with angel food cake squares, strawberries, orange sections, pineapple chunks and/or marshmallows.

# CHOCOLATE MOUSSE TERRINE

| | |
|---|---|
| 1 | cup semisweet chocolate chips |
| 2 | tablespoons sugar |
| 3 | tablespoons cold water |
| 3 | egg yolks, beaten |
| 3 | egg whites, stiffly beaten |
| 1 | teaspoon vanilla extract |
| 1 | cup whipping cream, whipped |
| 12 | ladyfingers, split lengthwise |

Combine the chocolate chips, sugar and water in a double boiler. Heat over hot, but not boiling, water until the chocolate melts and the mixture is smooth, stirring constantly. Stir a small amount of the hot mixture into the egg yolks. Stir the egg yolks into the hot mixture. Let stand until cooled.

Fold the egg whites into the chocolate mixture. Fold in the vanilla and whipped cream. Layer the ladyfingers and chocolate mixture alternately in a 5 × 7-inch pan. Chill, covered, for 24 hours. Cut into slices. Serve with whipped cream if desired.

*Serves eight*

## Cooking Tips

### ABOUT CHOCOLATE

Read the label when buying chocolate. If it does not contain cocoa butter, it is confectionery coating or white chocolate, which is not a true chocolate. Unaltered chocolate is marketed as unsweetened, baking, or bitter chocolate. The addition of sugar, lecithin, and vanilla creates bittersweet, semisweet, or sweet chocolate, depending on the amount of sugar. Milk chocolate contains at least 12 percent milk solids and 10 percent chocolate liquor.

# BANANA SOFT TACOS WITH PAPAYA SAUCE

**Tacos**

| | |
|---|---|
| 2 | cups flour, sifted twice |
| 1 | tablespoon sugar |
| 1/8 | teaspoon salt |
| 1 | cup milk |
| 2 | eggs, beaten |
| 2 | egg yolks, beaten |
| 1/4 | cup (1/2 stick) unsalted butter, melted |
| 2 | tablespoons Cognac |

**Filling**

| | |
|---|---|
| 1/4 | cup (1/2 stick) unsalted butter |
| 1/2 | cup plus 2 tablespoons packed brown sugar |
| 1 | tablespoon freshly squeezed orange juice |
| 1 | tablespoon Grand Marnier |
| 3 | medium bananas, cut into 1/2-inch-thick slices |
| 1/2 | pint strawberries, hulled |

**Papaya Sauce**

| | |
|---|---|
| 1 | papaya, peeled, halved, seeded |
| 3 | tablespoons sugar |
| 1 | teaspoon cinnamon |

*For the tacos*, combine the flour, sugar and salt in a bowl and mix well. Beat in the milk, eggs and egg yolks gradually. Stir in the melted butter and Cognac. Let stand for 15 to 20 minutes. Butter an 8-inch sauté pan lightly. Pour 2 tablespoons of the batter into the pan and swirl to coat the bottom. Cook over medium heat for 2 to 3 minutes or until light brown. Turn and cook for an additional 1 to 2 minutes. Repeat the process until all the batter is used, stacking the cooked tortillas between sheets of waxed paper.

*For the filling*, heat the butter and 1/2 cup of the brown sugar in a saucepan over medium heat until melted, stirring frequently. Stir in the orange juice and Grand Marnier. Cook over low heat for 5 minutes or until thickened, stirring occasionally. Remove from the heat. Add the bananas, stirring to coat. Cut half the strawberries into 1/2-inch pieces. Place in a bowl. Purée the remaining strawberries and remaining 2 tablespoons brown sugar in a blender. Pour over the strawberries and stir to combine.

*For the sauce*, cut a papaya half into 1/4-inch pieces. Purée the remaining papaya, sugar and cinnamon in a blender. Combine the puréed mixture and the papaya pieces in a bowl and mix well.

*To assemble*, place 6 to 8 banana slices in the center of each of 8 to 12 tortillas using a slotted spoon. Roll up loosely. Place 2 rolled tacos on each individual ovenproof serving plate. Brush a small amount of the liquid from the bananas over the tacos. Brown lightly under a preheated broiler. Divide the remaining banana slices among the tacos. Spoon the strawberry mixture next to the tacos. Serve with Papaya Sauce on the side.

*Serves four to six*

# CITRUS TIRAMISU

1/4 cup sugar

2 tablespoons Cognac or brandy

8 ounces fat-free cream cheese, softened

3 1/2 ounces mascarpone cheese

24 ladyfingers, split lengthwise

1 1/2 cups strong-brewed coffee

1 cup orange sections, chopped

1 teaspoon baking cocoa

Beat the sugar, Cognac, cream cheese and mascarpone cheese in a bowl until smooth. Dip the cut sides of 12 ladyfingers in the coffee. Arrange cut side down in rows in an 8 × 8-inch dish. Dip the flat sides of 12 ladyfingers in the coffee. Arrange over the layer of ladyfingers. Spread half the cheese mixture and half the chopped oranges over the ladyfingers. Layer with the remaining cheese mixture and oranges. Chill for 8 hours. Sprinkle with the baking cocoa.

*Serves eight*

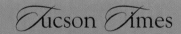

## ELECTRIC CARS

General Motors selected Tucson as one of four cities in the country in which to introduce the EV1, an electric car. Specially marked blue parking spaces are reserved for electric cars and offer recharging stations.

# MACADAMIA-CRUSTED PEAR TORTE

**Crust**

1 1/2 cups flour
1/2 cup (1 stick) butter,
    melted
1 1/2 cups sugar
1/2 cup chopped
    macadamia nuts

**Filling**

8 ounces cream cheese,
    softened
1/4 cup sugar
1 egg
1 teaspoon vanilla extract
2 pears, peeled, cut
    into slices
1 teaspoon apple pie spice
1 teaspoon fresh
    lemon juice
1/4 cup sugar

*For the crust,* combine the flour, butter, sugar and mcadamia nuts in a bowl and mix well. Press over the bottom and side of an 8-inch tart pan. Bake at 350 degrees for 12 minutes or until the crust begins to brown. Set aside to cool. Increase the oven temperature to 400 degrees.

*For the filling,* combine the cream cheese, 1/4 cup sugar, egg and vanilla in a bowl and mix well. Pour into the prepared pan. Combine the pears, pie spice, lemon juice and 1/4 cup sugar in a bowl and toss to coat the pears. Arrange the pears in a circle over the cream cheese filling. Pour any remaining liquid over the top. Bake for 20 to 25 minutes or until set.

*Serves eight to ten*

# CHOCOLATE DECADENCE

1    pound dark sweet
     chocolate
5    ounces unsalted butter
4    eggs
1    tablespoon sugar
1    tablespoon flour
12 to 16 ounces fresh
     raspberries or frozen
     raspberries, thawed,
     drained
4    ounces dark sweet
     chocolate
2    cups whipping cream
1    tablespoon
     confectioners' sugar
1    teaspoon vanilla extract

Cut a circle of baking parchment or waxed paper to fit the bottom of an 8-inch cake pan. Place in the pan.

Combine 1 pound dark chocolate and butter in a microwave-safe dish or double boiler. Microwave in the dish or heat over simmering water until melted, stirring to mix.

Combine the eggs and sugar in a double boiler. Heat over simmering water just until barely warm to the touch, whisking to dissolve the sugar. Remove from the heat and beat at high speed until the eggs are of the consistency of lightly whipped cream.

Fold in the flour. Mix 1/3 of the egg mixture into the melted chocolate. Fold the chocolate mixture into the remaining eggs and stir until smooth. Pour into the prepared pan and tap to settle evenly.

Bake at 425 degrees for 15 minutes. Place the pan with the cake in the freezer until chilled, or freeze for up to 1 month.

Purée the raspberries in a food processor or blender. Strain to remove the seeds. Draw a vegetable peeler across the remaining 4 ounces dark chocolate to make curls. Whip the cream with the confectioners' sugar and vanilla in a mixing bowl until soft peaks form.

Remove the baked layer from the freezer and rotate the pan quickly over high heat to loosen. Remove to a serving plate and remove the parchment. Mound the whipped cream on top and sprinkle with the chocolate curls. Chill, covered, until 15 minutes before serving. Cut into slices and serve with a dollop of raspberry purée.

*Serves eight*

# CHOCOLATE MALT CAKE

## Cake

1 2/3 cups flour
2/3 cup malted milk powder
1 1/2 teaspoons baking
powder
1/4 teaspoon baking soda
1/2 teaspoon salt
3/4 cup (1 1/2 sticks) butter,
softened
1 1/3 cups sugar
3 eggs
1 1/2 teaspoons vanilla
extract
3 ounces unsweetened
chocolate, melted
1 1/4 cups plus
2 tablespoons milk

## Frosting

1 cup (2 sticks) butter,
softened
1 teaspoon vanilla extract
2 tablespoons milk
1/4 cup baking cocoa
1 1/4 cups confectioners'
sugar
1/2 cup malted milk balls,
chopped

*For the cake*, butter and flour a 9 × 13-inch cake pan.
Combine the flour, malted milk powder, baking powder,
baking soda and salt in a bowl and mix well. Cream the
butter and sugar in a mixing bowl until light and fluffy.
Beat in the eggs 1 at a time, mixing well after each
addition. Beat in the vanilla and chocolate. Add the flour
mixture alternately with the milk, mixing well after each
addition. Pour into the prepared pan. Bake at 350 degrees
for 35 minutes or until a wooden pick inserted in the
center comes out clean.

*For the frosting*, beat the butter with the vanilla in a
bowl until smooth. Beat in the milk, baking cocoa and
confectioners' sugar. Spread over the cake. Sprinkle the
candy over the top.

*Serves sixteen*

## Tucson Times

### CREOSOTE BUSH

The creosote bush is
by far the most
common shrub in the
Southwest. After a
summer rain, its
clean, pungent aroma
mingled with wet
dust wafts of the
desert, sweetening
the air. Native
Americans have long
used its leaves for
medicinal purposes.

# GUILT-FREE CHOCOLATE CAKE

1³/4 cups flour
2 cups sugar
³/4 cup baking cocoa
1¹/2 teaspoons baking soda
1¹/2 teaspoons baking
powder
4 egg whites
1 cup skim milk
¹/2 cup unsweetened
applesauce
2 teaspoons vanilla
extract
1 cup boiling water
¹/4 cup confectioners'
sugar

Combine the flour, sugar, baking cocoa, baking soda and baking powder in a mixing bowl and mix well. Add the egg whites, skim milk, applesauce and vanilla. Beat at medium speed for 2 minutes. Stir in the boiling water. Pour into a 9 × 13-inch baking pan sprayed with nonstick cooking spray.

Bake at 350 degrees for 35 to 40 minutes or until a wooden pick inserted in the center comes out clean. Cool on a wire rack. Sift the confectioners' sugar over the cake.

Serves sixteen

# OATMEAL CAKE

## Cake

1 1/2 cups boiling water
1  cup quick-cooking oats
1/2  cup (1 stick) margarine
1  cup sugar
2  eggs
1  teaspoon baking soda
1  teaspoon salt
1  cup packed brown
   sugar
1 1/2 cups sifted flour
1  teaspoon cinnamon

## Frosting

1  cup packed brown
   sugar
1/2  cup shredded coconut
1/2  teaspoon vanilla extract
2  tablespoons margarine,
   softened
1/4  cup evaporated milk

*For the cake*, combine the boiling water, oats and margarine in a bowl and mix well. Let stand, covered, for 20 minutes. Add the sugar, eggs, baking soda, salt, brown sugar, flour and cinnamon and mix well. Spoon into a 9 × 13-inch baking pan. Bake at 350 degrees for 35 minutes.

*For the frosting*, combine the brown sugar, coconut, vanilla, margarine and evaporated milk in a bowl and mix well. Spread over the hot cake. Broil for 2 minutes.

*Serves twelve*

# ORANGE DATE CAKE

## Cake
1/4    cup all-purpose flour
2    cups chopped dates
1    cup chopped walnuts
4    cups sifted cake flour
2    teaspoons baking soda
1    cup (2 sticks) butter
2    cups sugar
4    eggs
1/4    cup grated orange zest

## Glaze
1    cup sugar
1/4    cup grated orange zest
1    cup (about)
     orange juice

*For the cake*, spray a bundt pan or 3 loaf pans with nonstick cooking spray. Dust with the all-purpose flour. Combine the dates, walnuts and a small amount of cake flour in a bowl and toss to coat. Set aside.

Sift the cake flour and baking soda together. Cream the butter and sugar in a mixing bowl until light and fluffy. Beat in the eggs 1 at a time. Beat in the orange zest. Beat in the sifted dry ingredients gradually. Stir in the dates and walnuts. Pour into the prepared pan. Draw a knife through the batter. Bake at 350 degrees for 45 to 55 minutes or until a wooden pick inserted in the center comes out clean. Invert onto a serving plate.

*For the glaze*, combine the sugar, orange zest and enough orange juice to make of the desired consistency in a saucepan. Cook over low heat until warm, stirring frequently. Glaze the hot cake.

*Serves sixteen*

# ARIZONA INN

The Arizona Inn, with its flamingo-colored stucco, is a Tucson landmark and a favorite spot for locals to celebrate weddings, anniversaries, and family reunions. The homey decor, intimate surroundings, and lush garden setting in the middle of a residential neighborhood have attracted Hollywood stars, political dignitaries, and everyday travelers alike. Isabella Greenway opened the Arizona Inn in 1932, in part to house furniture built by the Arizona Hut. The Hut was a charity organization started by Isabella in 1927 as a way of helping and employing disabled ex-servicemen in the design and construction of furniture. Isabella was a true pioneer, and was not only one of the first women to hold a congressional seat in Arizona, but was one of the founding members of the Junior League of Tucson.

# CLASSIC RUM CAKE

### Cake
1   cup chopped pecans
1   (2-layer) package
    yellow cake mix
1/2   cup vegetable oil
1/2   cup rum
1/2   cup water
4   eggs
1   (4-ounce) package
    vanilla instant
    pudding mix

### Rum Sauce
1/4   cup (1/2 stick) butter
1/4   cup sugar
1/4   cup rum
1/4   cup water

*For the cake*, sprinkle the pecans over the bottom of a greased and floured bundt pan. Combine the cake mix, oil, rum, water, eggs and pudding mix in a mixing bowl. Beat at medium speed for 5 minutes. Pour into the prepared pan. Bake for 50 to 60 minutes or until golden brown. Cool for 5 minutes. Invert onto a serving plate.

*For the sauce*, combine the butter, sugar, rum and water in a saucepan. Bring to a boil, stirring frequently. Boil for 2 minutes. Cool for 30 minutes. Pour over the hot cake.

*Serves sixteen*

# SOUR CREAM CAKE

1   cup sour cream
1/4   teaspoon baking soda
3   cups sugar
1   cup (2 sticks) butter,
    softened
6   eggs, *at room*
    *temperature*
1   tablespoon vanilla
    *extract*
3   cups flour

Combine the sour cream and baking soda in a bowl and mix well. Cream the sugar and butter in a mixing bowl until light and fluffy. Add the sour cream mixture and mix well. Add the eggs 1 at a time, mixing well after each addition. Add the vanilla and mix well. Add the flour 1 cup at a time, mixing well after each addition. Pour into a bundt pan. Bake at 325 degrees for 1 1/2 hours. Serve with fresh peaches or strawberries.

*Serves ten*

# TEXAS SHEET CAKE

## Cake

| | |
|---|---|
| 1/2 | cup milk |
| 1 | tablespoon white or cider vinegar |
| 2 | cups sugar |
| 2 | cups flour |
| 1 | teaspoon baking soda |
| 1/2 | cup (1 stick) butter |
| 1 | cup water |
| 1/2 | cup vegetable oil |
| 1/4 | cup baking cocoa |
| 2 | eggs |
| 1/2 | teaspoon cinnamon |

## Frosting

| | |
|---|---|
| 1/2 | cup (1stick) butter |
| 1/4 | cup baking cocoa |
| 6 | tablespoons milk |
| 1 | teaspoon vanilla extract |
| 1 | (1-pound) package confectioners' sugar |

*For the cake*, combine the milk and vinegar in a small bowl. Let stand for 10 minutes. Combine the sugar, flour and baking soda in a large bowl and mix well. Combine the butter, water, oil and baking cocoa in a saucepan. Bring to a boil over medium heat, stirring constantly. Pour over the dry ingredients and mix well. Add the milk mixture, eggs and cinnamon and mix well. Pour into a greased 10 × 15-inch baking pan. Bake at 400 degrees for 20 to 25 minutes or until the cake tests done. Set on a wire rack to cool slightly.

*For the frosting*, combine the butter, baking cocoa, milk and vanilla in a saucepan. Bring to a boil, stirring constantly. Remove from the heat. Stir in the confectioners' sugar. Beat with an electric mixer until smooth. Spread the frosting on the warm cake.

*Serves twenty*

## About Thyme

### EDIBLE FLOWERS

Flowers can be used as ingredients as well as garnishes. The most flavorful flowers are the blossoms of chives, calendulas, day lilies, marigolds, mint, nasturtiums, pansies, roses, sage, squash blossoms, or sweet borage. Carnations, chrysanthemums, nasturtiums, and marigolds can be added to salads.

# CHOCOLATE ALMOND BISCOTTI

2    cups flour
1    cup sugar
1/3  cup baking cocoa
1    teaspoon baking soda
1/4  teaspoon salt
2    eggs
2    egg whites
3/4  teaspoon vanilla extract
2/3  cup slivered almonds,
       toasted
1/3  cup chocolate chips
1    egg, beaten

Combine the flour, sugar, baking cocoa, baking soda and salt in a mixing bowl. Combine the eggs, egg whites and vanilla in a bowl and mix well. Add to the flour mixture gradually, beating at low speed. Combine the almonds and chocolate chips in a small bowl and toss to combine. Stir into the batter.

Shape the dough into two 2-inch-diameter logs on a floured surface. Place on a greased baking sheet. Brush with the beaten egg.

Bake at 350 degrees for 30 to 35 minutes or until golden brown. Cool for 15 minutes. Cut into slices diagonally. Place the slices on a greased baking sheet.

Bake at 350 degrees for 15 to 20 minutes or until toasted. Let stand until cooled. Store in an airtight container.

*Serves twenty-four*

# CHOCOLATE CRINKLES

2    cups flour
2    teaspoons baking
     powder
1/2  teaspoon salt
1/2  cup (1 stick) butter
1    teaspoon instant coffee
     (optional)
4    ounces unsweetened
     chocolate, coarsely
     chopped
2    cups sugar
4    eggs
1 1/2 teaspoons vanilla
     extract
1    cup confectioners'
     sugar

Mix together the flour, baking powder and salt. Combine the butter, coffee granules and chocolate in a double boiler. Heat over hot, but not boiling, water until melted, stirring frequently. Beat the chocolate mixture and sugar in a mixing bowl at medium speed until blended. Add the eggs 1 at a time, mixing well after each addition. Beat in the vanilla. Beat in the flour mixture at low speed just until blended. Chill for 2 hours or until firm.

Shape the chilled dough by teaspoonfuls into balls. Drop into the confectioners' sugar to coat. Place 2 inches apart on a greased cookie sheet. Bake at 350 degrees for 10 to 12 minutes or until the tops of the cookies are just set; do not overbake. Cool on the cookie sheet for 1 minute. Remove to a wire rack and cool completely.

*Serves sixty*

## Cooking Tips

### CRACKING PECANS

To crack pecans easily, cover them with water in a saucepan and bring to a boil. Let stand, covered, until cool; drain. Blot the pecans dry, position the nutcracker at the ends of the pecan, and crack. Store shelled pecans in a cool dry place for several months or for up to one year in the freezer. Two pounds of unshelled pecans will yield one pound of shelled pecans or four cups whole pecans.

# GINGER CRINKLE COOKIES

2/3   cup vegetable oil
1     egg
1/4   cup molasses
1     cup sugar
2     cups flour
2     teaspoons baking soda
1/2   teaspoon salt
1     teaspoon cinnamon
1     teaspoon ginger
Sugar for coating

Combine the oil, egg, molasses, 1 cup sugar, flour, baking soda, salt, cinnamon and ginger in a bowl and mix well. Shape the dough by tablespoonfuls into balls. Roll in the sugar to coat. Place on a cookie sheet. Press with a fork. Bake at 350 degrees for 10 to 15 minutes or until the cookies begin to brown. Cool on a wire rack.

*Serves twenty-four*

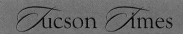

## Tucson Times

### TUCSON'S CLIMATE

The temperature in Tucson fluctuates from 110 to 65 degrees in the daytime and from just above freezing to 85 degrees at night, with few nights dipping below 32 degrees. The daytime temperature during the 60 to 90 days of summer averages 99.5 degrees and nights average 75 degrees. The average rainfall fluctuates between 6 and 12 inches a year.

# OATMEAL AND
# WHITE CHOCOLATE CHIP COOKIES

1    cup (2 sticks) butter,
     softened
1    cup packed brown
     sugar
1/2  cup sugar
2    eggs
1    teaspoon vanilla extract
1    teaspoon baking soda
1/2 to 1 cup pecans
3/4  cup flour
3    cups rolled oats
2    cups white
     chocolate chips

Combine the butter, brown sugar, sugar, eggs and vanilla in a bowl and mix well. Add the baking soda, pecans, flour, oats and white chocolate chips and mix well. Drop by teaspoonfuls onto a cookie sheet. Bake at 350 degrees for 7 to 10 minutes or until the cookies begin to brown. Cool on a wire rack.

*Serves thirty*

# MONSTER COOKIES

12   eggs
1    (2-pound) package
     brown sugar
4    cups sugar
1    tablespoon vanilla
     extract
1    tablespoon light
     corn syrup
8    teaspoons baking soda
2    cups (4 sticks) butter,
     softened
4    (12-ounce) jars
     peanut butter
18   cups rolled oats
2²/3 cups chocolate chips
Milk (optional)
1    pound "M&M's" Plain
     Chocolate Candies

Combine the eggs, brown sugar, sugar, vanilla and corn syrup in a large bowl and mix well. Add the baking soda, butter and peanut butter and mix well. Add the oats and chocolate chips and toss gently to combine. Add enough milk to make a moist batter. Drop by ice cream scoopfuls onto an ungreased cookie sheet, approximately 6 to a sheet. Flatten with a spatula. Arrange the "M&M's" on the top.

Bake in a preheated 350-degree oven for 12 minutes; do not overbake. Cool on the cookie sheet for 1 minute. Remove to a wire rack to cool completely. May substitute coconut and sliced almonds for the "M&M's".

*Serves one hundred*

# PEANUT BUTTER BARS

## Cookies

- ¹/₂  cup (1 stick) butter, softened
- ¹/₂  cup sugar
- ¹/₂  cup packed brown sugar
- 1  egg
- ¹/₃  cup peanut butter
- ¹/₂  teaspoon baking soda
- ¹/₄  teaspoon salt
- ¹/₂  teaspoon vanilla extract
- 1  cup flour
- 1  cup quick-cooking oats
- 1  cup chocolate chips

## Frosting

- ¹/₂  cup confectioners' sugar
- ¹/₄  cup peanut butter
- Milk

*For the cookies*, cream the butter, sugar and brown sugar in a mixing bowl until light and fluffy. Add the egg, peanut butter, baking soda, salt and vanilla and mix well. Stir in the flour and oats. Spread evenly in a greased 9 × 13-inch baking pan. Bake at 350 degrees for 20 minutes. Sprinkle the chocolate chips over the top, spreading evenly as they melt. Let stand until cooled and chocolate is hardened.

*For the frosting*, combine the confectioners' sugar and peanut butter in a bowl and mix well. Add enough milk to make of a spreading consistency. Spread over the cooled chocolate layer. Cut into bars to serve.

*Serves fifteen*

# MELT AWAY SHORTBREAD

$2^1/4$ cups ($4^1/2$ sticks)
   butter, softened
$1^1/2$ cups sugar
$3^3/4$ cups all-purpose flour
$3/4$ cup rice flour
Sugar for sprinkling

Cream the butter and $1^1/2$ cups sugar in a mixing bowl until light and fluffy. Add the all-purpose flour and rice flour and mix well. Knead until the mixture forms a ball. Press evenly over the bottom of an 11 × 17-inch baking pan. Prick many times with a fork.

Bake at 275 degrees for 1 to $1^1/4$ hours or until a light golden brown. Cut the hot shortbread into 1 × $3^1/2$-inch pieces. Sprinkle with sugar. Remove from the pan and place on a brown paper grocery bag. Let stand until cooled.

*Serves forty-eight*

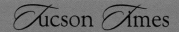

### BIOSPHERE 2

Biosphere 2 is the world's first miniature biosphere and the world's largest glass-enclosed ecological laboratory. It is located north of Tucson in the foothills of the Santa Catalina Mountains. The ocean in Biosphere 2 is the largest human-made ocean in the world. Its fish and other life can be viewed from an underwater viewing gallery. While researchers lived for years in the ecological laboratory, tours were limited to the exterior. Now visitors are permitted to go inside to see how this miniature of our own biosphere operates.

# NEW ENGLAND APPLE PIE

### Pie Pastry
2   cups flour
1   teaspoon salt
2/3   cup plus 2 tablespoons
     shortening
4 to 5 tablespoons cold
     water

### Apple Filling
3/4   cup sugar
1/4   cup flour
1/2   teaspoon nutmeg
1/2   teaspoon cinnamon
Dash of salt
4   McIntosh apples,
     peeled, cut into slices
2   Granny Smith apples,
     peeled, cut into slices
2   tablespoons margarine

*For the pie pastry,* combine the flour and salt in a bowl. Cut in the shortening until crumbly. Add the water 1 tablespoon at a time, mixing with a fork until the mixture forms a ball. Chill, wrapped in plastic wrap, for 30 minutes or longer. Divide into 2 portions. Roll 1 portion into an 11-inch circle on a lightly floured surface. Fit into a 9-inch pie plate. Roll the remaining portion into a 10-inch circle on a lightly floured surface.

*For the pie filling,* combine the sugar, flour, nutmeg, cinnamon and salt in a bowl and mix well. Add the apple slices and toss to coat. Spoon into the pastry-lined pie plate. Dot with the margarine. Top with the remaining pastry, sealing the edge and cutting 6 vents. Cover the edge with a 3-inch strip of foil. Bake at 425 degrees for 25 minutes. Remove the foil strip. Bake for 15 to 25 minutes longer or until the crust is brown and the juice is bubbly.

*Serves six to eight*

---

## Cooking Tips

### ABOUT APPLES

An apple a day may very well keep the doctor away. An apple delivers about 43 grams of dietary fiber, about as much as two slices of whole wheat bread. Apples are also good sources of potassium, which protects against strokes, and boron, which may help prevent the loss of calcium from bone. They are low in sodium, calories, and fat—so eat up!

# MARGARITA PIE

**Pretzel Pie Pastry**
   $1^1/2$ cups crushed pretzels
   $1^1/2$ cups sugar
   $1/2$   cup (1 stick) butter,
       softened

**Filling**
   3    cups whipping cream
   $3/4$   cup sugar
   $1^1/2$ tablespoons bottled
       lime juice
   3    tablespoons Triple Sec
   $1/2$   cup tequila
   $3/4$   cup sugar
   Juice of 2 limes
   Juice of 1 orange
   $1/8$   teaspoon salt
   1     envelope unflavored
       gelatin

*For the pie pastry*, combine the pretzels, sugar and butter in a bowl and mix well. Press over the bottoms and up the sides of two 9-inch pie plates.

*For the filling*, whip the cream in a mixing bowl until soft peaks form. Beat in $3/4$ cup sugar gradually, beating until stiff peaks form. Refrigerate until ready to use. Combine the bottled lime juice, Triple Sec, tequila, $3/4$ cup sugar, lime juice, orange juice and salt and mix well. Add the gelatin to soften. Pour the gelatin mixture into a double boiler. Cook until the gelatin is dissolved. Let stand for 1 hour; do not chill. Fold into the whipped cream. Spoon into the pie shells. Freeze, covered, until ready to serve. Garnish with lime slices.

*Serves twenty-four*

# OLD-FASHIONED PECAN PIE

**Basic Pie Pastry**

1¹/3  cups flour
1  teaspoon sugar
¹/4  teaspoon salt
¹/3  cup shortening, chilled,
     cut into small pieces
¹/4  cup (¹/2 stick) unsalted
     butter, chilled, cut into
     small pieces
2  tablespoons (about)
   ice water

**Filling**

1  cup sugar
3  eggs
¹/2  cup light corn syrup
3  tablespoons unsalted
   butter, melted
2  teaspoons vanilla
   extract
1³/4 cups chopped pecans

*For the pastry,* combine the flour, sugar and salt in a food processor container. Add the shortening and butter and pulse until crumbly. Add the ice water gradually, pulsing until the mixture forms moist balls. Chill, wrapped with plastic wrap, for 1 hour or longer. Roll into a 13-inch circle on a lightly floured surface. Fit into a 9-inch round baking pan with a 1¹/2-inch side. Trim even with the pan edge. Freeze for 15 minutes.

*For the filling,* whisk the sugar, eggs, corn syrup, butter and vanilla in a bowl. Stir in ³/4 cup of the pecans. Spoon into the pastry-lined pan. Sprinkle with the remaining 1 cup pecans. Bake at 350 degrees for 1¹/4 hours or until set. Cool on a wire rack.

*Serves eight*

## Other Temptations

### SIMPLE PIE PASTRY

Sift 5 cups flour, 1 teaspoon salt and ¹/2 teaspoon baking powder into a bowl. Beat 1 egg with 1 tablespoon vinegar in a measuring cup. Add enough water to measure ³/4 cup. Cut 1 pound of shortening into the flour mixture until crumbly. Add the egg mixture and mix to form a dough. Use immediately or freeze for later use.

# SPICED PUMPKIN PIE

1   medium pie pumpkin,
    or 2 cups pumpkin
    purée
2/3  cup packed brown
    sugar
1/2  cup sugar
1   tablespoon flour
1/2  teaspoon salt
1/8  teaspoon freshly
    ground pepper
1 1/2 teaspoons cinnamon
1/2  teaspoon freshly grated
    nutmeg
1/2  teaspoon ground ginger
1/4  teaspoon allspice
1   cup heavy cream
1/3  cup milk
2   eggs, lightly beaten
1 1/2 teaspoons vanilla
    extract
3   tablespoons bourbon
    or rum
1   (9-inch) deep-dish
    pie shell
Whipped cream

Cover a baking sheet with foil. Cut the pumpkin into halves horizontally. Place cut side down on the prepared baking sheet. Place foil over the pumpkin in a tent shape. Bake at 350 degrees for 1 1/2 hours. Let stand until cooled. Remove the seeds. Scoop the pulp into a food processor container and purée.

Whisk 2 cups of the pumpkin purée, brown sugar, sugar, flour, salt, pepper, cinnamon, nutmeg, ginger, allspice, cream, milk, eggs, vanilla and bourbon in a large bowl. Pour into the pie shell.

Bake at 400 degrees for 45 minutes or until the filling is almost set in the center. Cool on a wire rack. Serve with whipped cream.

*Serves eight*

# Acknowledgements

We gratefully acknowledge the generous donations from
the following individuals and companies:

Janet Vasilius
Virginia Greene Kat

Debbie Altschul
Cindy Barrett
Bentley's House of Coffee & Tea
Berwick-Himes Insurance Services, LLC
In Memory of Nelly Baxter Bruce
Audrey & James Campbell
Jennifer A. Casteix
Diane Marie Ceizyk
Centerline Design & Construction, Inc.
Citizens Transfer & Storage Co., Inc.
Christopher & Mary Clements
Elizabeth C. Cohn
In Memory of Persis Browne Congdon
Dr. J. Wright & Virgie Cortner
Tana & Robert Curtis
Debbie Davis
Mary Kay & Philip Dinsmore

Elements—Home Accessories & Gifts
Lynn & George Feulner
Kimberly & Marty Flack
Claire Genser
Mary J. Greene
Jennifer & Tim Harris
Heidi H. Hildreth
Stephanie & Bryan Hudson
Natalie Ireland
JLT 1999–2000 Underwriting Committee
Ann H. Johnson
Deborah Johnson
Pamela & William Kane
Peg H. Kepner
Adaline Klemmedson
Sally Lanyon
Katherine Rose McLaughlin
Emily B. Minerich
Grace & Jim Murphy

Dr. Jeffrey Nelson
Louis A. & Sharon D. Norman
Karen & Gene Palmour
Marty & Peter Pritz
Patty E. Rader
Kathleen Rector-Wyckoff
Stacia & Peter Reko
Executive Chef Bruce Rogers,
    Viscount Suite Hotel
Tiana & Jeff Ronstadt
Scott Rumel, Architect
Jenn Staples
Kathleen & Tom Stevenson,
    Pusch Ridge Software
Rebecca & Jerry Sundt
Brenda Tolle & Joan Tolle
Susan Villarreal
Laura & Ray Wallace
Kristin Wellik
Megan Wood

## THE JUNIOR LEAGUE OF TUCSON, INC.
### ACTIVE MEMBERS 1998–1999

Amy Ahler
Carolyn Andersen
Terry Bailey
Suzanne Baron
Heather Beaty
Elizabeth Belton
Kerrin Berwick
Ieva Bilsens
Molly Bland
Stephanie Blonsky
Sally Bockisch
Cynthia Bozik
KarinAnne Breitlow
Jennifer Brumley
April Burge
Diane Cameron

Audrey Campbell
Jennifer A. Casteix
Diane Ceizyk
Jennifer Clark
Mary Clements
Stacie Cohen
Margaret Cole
Cynthia Combs
Sarah Congdon
Ann-Eve Cunningham
Tana Curtis
Susan Deaton
Carol Dietz
Elizabeth Doucette
Deana Duin
Kimberly Faber

Sheryl R. Ferranti-Hamza
Kimberly Flack
Michele Foutz
Kathryn Gastelum
Holly G. Griffith
Lisa Groeger
Amy Groh
Carey Hall
Janet Hare
Jennifer Harris
Junna Hayashi
Jenn Haynes
Dani Hemmings
Kristin Highton
Jeanne Hoover
Amy Jo Horner

Stephanie Hudson
Jimmie Huebner
Nicole James
Kathleen E. Jensen
Michelle Jenson
Jody E. Jepson
Jennifer Johnson
Pamela Kane
Ainsley Kellar
Sondra Kennedy
Elizabeth King
Amy Kleindienst
Tobie Kreiner
Melissa Larson
Gail Susan Lehmann
April Leonard

Andrea Lewis
Marilee Lorenz
Toni Lowry
Carol Ann Maitland
Sandra Maltry
Kristine Marsh
Nancy McKearney
Kelly McLaughlin
Mindy Mele
Lisa Miller
Diana Miner
Mollie Minke
Poe Minton
Lisa Marie Monjer
Heidi Montijo
Julie Muehlebach
Cherie D. Murphy
Lisa Murphy
Elizabeth Ann Naughton

Karen Nelson
Karlene Nelson
Sharon Norman
Marie O'Brien
Deirdre O'Brien-Montijo
Kathryn Olson
Deborah O'Hara
Suzy Ostrem
Harriet H. Parish
Jessica Pennebaker
Julie Peters
Jean Popham
Martha Pritz
Jennifer Quis
Patty E. Rader
Lenn Rainwater
Jill Reilly
Sacha L. Reilly
Nicole Reimers

Stacia Reko
Lisa Renteria
Margaret Richardson
Jennifer Riden
Kathleen Roberts-Stevenson
Tiana Ronstadt
Margo Rooney
Robin L. Rosema
Tracey Rowley
Tiffany Rumel
Nancy Russell
Tracy Shake
Betsey Shepard
Kym Slone
Kristie Stevens
Susan Stoll
Kimberly Sundt
Rebecca J. Sundt
Shamra Tankersley

Diane Tober
Brenda Tolle
Dawn Vandaveer
Laura Wallace
Sara Wallace
Christina Watkins
Susan Weeks
Kristin Wellik
Elizabeth White
Polly White
Tamra Williamson
Elizabeth Wilson
Ruthann Witkop
Megan Wood
Kelly Wyland
Lynda Zimmermann

## THE JUNIOR LEAGUE OF TUCSON, INC.
### WISHES TO THANK THESE FRIENDS WHO ASSISTED WITH GATHERING AND TESTING RECIPES

Rita Aigner
Claire Albanese
Deborah Altschul
Roberta Barg
Eleanor Barkley
Joyce Becker
Faye Blake
Judith Bland
Patti Borden
Debbie Brenton

Vickie Butler
Melinda Carrell
Joanne Collins
Betty Jo Drachman
Susan Flynn
Elizabeth Hastings
Kathryn Heineman
Geneva Heller
Freddy Hershberger
Jean D. Hills

Deborah Johnson
Charlotte Kirchner
Dian Lieberthal Rutin
Betsy Marshall
Lynette Matteson
Ann McCalley
Katherine McDonough
Catherine Mendelsohn
Elisa Michaels
Grace Murphy

Jody Owens
Marilyn Rutschman
Helen Schannep
Carolyn Shultz
Vicki Stanton
Mary Margaret Van Slyck
Susan Villarreal
Diana Warren
Meredith Weedin
Phyllis Wenger

## CREDITS

Lockard, Peggy Hamilton: *This is Tucson: Guidebook to the Old Pueblo;* Pepper Publishing, 1983.

*Food and Prop Stylist:* Mary Seger.

Landmark Photography: Edward McCain, McCain Photography, pages 20, 40, 64, 92, 114, 136, 154, 178, 212, 232.

Food Photography: Thomas Veneklasen, pages 8, 32, 56, 80, 104, 124, 144, 166, 192, 218.

*Accessories in food photography provided by Table Talk and American Home Furnishings*

# NUTRITIONAL INFORMATION

Persons with dietary or health problems or whose diets require close monitoring should not rely solely on the nutritional information provided. They should consult their physician or a registered dietitian for specific information. The nutritional profile of these recipes is based on all measurements being level.

## Abbreviations for Nutritional Profile

Cal — Calories          T Fat — Total Fat          Sod — Sodium
Prot — Protein          Chol — Cholesterol         g — grams
Carbo — Carbohydrates   Fiber — Dietary Fiber      mg — milligrams

- Alcoholic ingredients have been analyzed for the basic information. Cooking causes the evaporation of alcohol, which decreases alcoholic and caloric content.
- Chicken, cooked for boning and chopping, has been roasted which yields the lowest caloric values.
- Cottage cheese is cream-style with 4.2 percent creaming mixture.
- Eggs are all large. Flour is unsifted all-purpose flour.
- Garnishes, serving suggestions, and other optional information and variations are not included in the profile.
- Margarine and butter are regular, not whipped or presoftened.
- Milk is whole milk, 3.5 percent butterfat. Low-fat milk is 1 percent butterfat. Evaporated milk is whole milk with 60 percent of the water removed.
- Oil is any type of vegetable cooking oil. Shortening is hydrogenated vegetable shortening.
- Salt and other ingredients to taste as noted in the ingredients have not been included.
- If a choice of ingredients has been given, the profile reflects the first option. If a choice of amounts has been given, the profile reflects the greater amount.

The recipes in this profile have been indicated with a ❧ symbol.

| Pg. No. | Recipe Title (Approx Per Serving) | Cal | Prot (g) | Carbo (g) | T Fat (g) | % Cal from Fat | Chol (mg) | Fiber (g) | Sod (mg) |
|---|---|---|---|---|---|---|---|---|---|
| 12 | Mushrooms Stuffed with Sun-Dried Tomatoes | 39 | 2 | 4 | 2 | 47 | 12 | 1 | 79 |
| 13 | Shallot Puffs | 23 | 1 | 2 | 1 | 52 | 20 | <1 | 26 |
| 14 | Chicken Tikka | 101 | 15 | <1 | 4 | 35 | 47 | <1 | 155 |
| 16 | Mussels in Cream Sauce | 379 | 41 | 14 | 14 | 35 | 114 | <1 | 682 |
| 17 | Seared Sea Scallops in Vodka and Leek Sauce | 182 | 11 | 4 | 9 | 47 | 51 | <1 | 513 |
| 22 | Roasted Tomato and Eggplant Crostini | 92 | 3 | 18 | 1 | 9 | 0 | 2 | 158 |
| 34 | Sopa de Albondigas | 257 | 19 | 17 | 12 | 42 | 90 | 1 | 461 |
| 39 | Curried Chicken and Thyme Soup | 469 | 42 | 61 | 5 | 9 | 98 | 4 | 1473 |
| 44 | Spicy Tropical Gazpacho | 103 | 1 | 26 | <1 | 3 | 0 | 2 | 400 |
| 49 | Southwest Cranberry Sauce | 69 | <1 | 16 | <1 | 1 | 0 | 1 | 2 |
| 52 | Mango Tomatillo Salsa | 77 | 1 | 18 | 1 | 8 | 0 | 3 | 4 |
| 53 | Pomegranate Salsa | 57 | 1 | 14 | <1 | 3 | 0 | 2 | 2 |
| 69 | Fresh Corn and Cilantro Salad | 130 | 4 | 24 | 4 | 22 | 0 | 4 | 92 |
| 76 | Mixed Greens and Mandarin Orange Salad | 242 | 4 | 27 | 14 | 51 | <1 | 2 | 147 |

| Pg. No. | Recipe Title (Approx Per Serving) | Cal | Prot (g) | Carbo (g) | T Fat (g) | % Cal from Fat | Chol (mg) | Fiber (g) | Sod (mg) |
|---|---|---|---|---|---|---|---|---|---|
| 77 | Millennium Waldorf Salad | 173 | 5 | 35 | 4 | 17 | 1 | 5 | 69 |
| 79 | Creamy Black Pepper Dressing | 24 | 1 | 1 | 2 | 59 | 1 | <1 | 15 |
| 85 | Sonoran Stew | 499 | 38 | 39 | 22 | 39 | 108 | 5 | 867 |
| 87 | Shredded Beef | 327 | 40 | <1 | 17 | 49 | 136 | <1 | 299 |
| 88 | Pastel de Choclo | 464 | 35 | 56 | 14 | 26 | 132 | 7 | 89 |
| 91 | Cabernet and Thyme Fillets of Beef | 547 | 48 | 3 | 28 | 48 | 172 | <1 | 320 |
| 101 | Caramelized Pork over Lettuce | 238 | 27 | 9 | 10 | 38 | 70 | 2 | 551 |
| 106 | Rosemary and Garlic Baked Chicken | 603 | 57 | 6 | 38 | 58 | 179 | 1 | 174 |
| 110 | Grilled Lemon Cinnamon Chicken | 297 | 54 | 4 | 6 | 20 | 146 | <1 | 133 |
| 110 | Honey-Baked Chicken | 354 | 54 | 18 | 6 | 16 | 146 | <1 | 282 |
| 113 | Moroccan Chicken Stew | 267 | 27 | 13 | 12 | 41 | 72 | 4 | 385 |
| 118 | Spicy Chicken with Black Bean Purée | 499 | 66 | 35 | 10 | 19 | 146 | 13 | 947 |
| 119 | Tex-Mex Chicken and Peppers | 223 | 21 | 18 | 8 | 33 | 42 | 6 | 925 |
| 127 | Tacos de Pescado | 331 | 17 | 19 | 20 | 55 | 50 | 3 | 246 |
| 128 | Citrus Red Snapper | 132 | 16 | 9 | 3 | 23 | 28 | 1 | 39 |
| 131 | Wine-Poached Salmon | 177 | 21 | 1 | 9 | 45 | 68 | <1 | 52 |
| 132 | Dilled Dijon Sea Bass | 205 | 23 | 2 | 2 | 15 | 51 | <1 | 1840 |
| 134 | Swordfish with Ginger and Lemon | 213 | 24 | 3 | 12 | 49 | 45 | 1 | 725 |
| 135 | Lemon and Basil Whitefish | 304 | 34 | 2 | 17 | 52 | 105 | <1 | 137 |
| 138 | Crab and Pasta Cakes | 182 | 13 | 12 | 8 | 44 | 98 | 1 | 293 |
| 142 | Shrimp with Tomatoes and Arugula | 146 | 18 | 3 | 7 | 42 | 157 | 1 | 194 |
| 149 | Flying Bow Tie Pasta | 595 | 42 | 68 | 17 | 26 | 81 | 5 | 218 |
| 150 | Orzo with Chicken and Peppers | 291 | 30 | 28 | 4 | 12 | 63 | 2 | 208 |
| 153 | Tequila Shrimp and Pasta | 559 | 22 | 89 | 9 | 15 | 64 | 3 | 83 |
| 156 | Linguini with Sweet Red Pepper Sauce | 296 | 11 | 56 | 5 | 14 | 2 | 6 | 458 |
| 159 | Penne with Asparagus and Pine Nuts | 430 | 17 | 54 | 17 | 35 | 7 | 5 | 308 |
| 168 | Greek-Style Green Beans | 122 | 5 | 23 | 3 | 19 | 0 | 8 | 22 |
| 170 | Lemon-Mustard Brussels Sprouts | 117 | 4 | 12 | 7 | 50 | 0 | 5 | 476 |
| 183 | Sunbelt Spinach | 166 | 6 | 14 | 12 | 57 | 0 | 4 | 99 |
| 184 | Spiced Butternut Squash | 176 | 3 | 24 | 8 | 39 | 0 | 7 | 73 |
| 188 | Oven-Roasted Vegetables | 213 | 4 | 36 | 7 | 29 | 0 | 4 | 313 |
| 189 | Antipasto Rice | 258 | 7 | 49 | 3 | 10 | 2 | 2 | 696 |
| 191 | Mango Ginger Rice | 203 | 4 | 41 | 2 | 9 | 0 | 1 | 199 |
| 201 | Lemon Ginger Muffins | 160 | 3 | 29 | 4 | 20 | <1 | 1 | 166 |
| 202 | Wheat Germ Muffins | 171 | 5 | 20 | 9 | 45 | 50 | 2 | 159 |
| 203 | Lemon Yogurt Pancakes | 97 | 4 | 17 | 2 | 17 | 30 | <1 | 165 |
| 203 | Pumpkin Clove Pancakes | 117 | 4 | 19 | 3 | 21 | 45 | 1 | 214 |
| 222 | Lemon Ice | 404 | 2 | 103 | 0 | 0 | 0 | <1 | 102 |
| 230 | Guilt-Free Chocolate Cake | 178 | 4 | 41 | 1 | 3 | <1 | 2 | 186 |

# Herb Chart

**Basil**  Member of the mint family with a strong, pungent, peppery flavor reminiscent of licorice and cloves. Popular in Mediterranean cooking, it is the main ingredient in pesto. It is also used in tomato dishes, poultry dishes, soups, and salad dressing.

**Bay Leaf**  The leaf of the laurel, seldom found fresh in markets. It imparts a lemon-nutmeg flavor and is widely used to flavor soups, stews, vegetables, and meats. Overuse can impart a bitter flavor.

**Bouquet Garni**  A French seasoning mix of fresh herbs, usually including parsley, thyme, and bay leaves, in addition to other herbs, spices, or vegetables. It is tied together and used to flavor stews, soups, and sauces.

**Chervil**  A mild-flavored member of the parsley family with elusive overtones of anise. It is one of the main ingredients in the *fines herbes* traditional to French cooking and is best used fresh.

**Chives**  A mild-flavored member of the onion family with hollow green stems and purple flowers, all of which are edible. Chives should be added to cooked dishes toward the end of the cooking time to retain flavor.

**Dill**  A member of the parsley family with a distinctive flavor that is easily lost during heating. It can be used to flavor salads, vegetables, meats, and sauces.

**Fennel**  Florence fennel is a perennial plant with foliage used in salads, stews, and soups and with a bulb cooked as a vegetable. Its flavor is similar to, but sweeter and more elusive than, anise. Common fennel is the variety from which seeds are harvested to use in both sweet and savory dishes.

**Garlic**  A member of the lily family and cousin to leeks, chives, onions, and shallots. Its highly aromatic flavor is used in most of the cuisines of the world. Pressing releases more of its essential oils than slicing.

**Marjoram**  A member of the mint family with a sweet flavor reminiscent of thyme and oregano, a strong aroma, and a cool aftertaste. It is used to flavor lamb, veal, and vegetables.

**Mint**  An aromatic family of herbs with over 30 species. It is used in both savory and sweet dishes, beverages, and as a garnish. Some of the species have flavors reminiscent of fruits, such as lemon, or other flavorings, such as chocolate.

**Oregano**  A member of the mint family, also known as wild marjoram, with a pungent, peppery flavor. It is especially good in dishes with a tomato foundation and in combination with basil.

**Parsley**  A mild herb with a slightly peppery, tangy flavor. Flat-leaf parsley is more strongly flavored than the curly-leaf variety. It is widely used as a flavor enhancer or garnish.

**Rosemary**  A member of the mint family with a strong flavor reminiscent of lemon and pine and a strong, sharp, camphorlike aroma. It is used as a seasoning for fruit salads, soups, poultry, lamb, fish, and egg dishes.

**Sage**  Native to the Mediterranean, with a slightly bitter, musty, mint flavor, and used for both medicinal and culinary purposes. It is commonly used in dishes containing pork, cheese, or beans, and in stuffings.

**Savory**  A relative of the mint family with a flavor and aroma reminiscent of a cross between thyme and mint. Winter savory has a more bitter and pungent flavor. It is used in pâtés, soups, meat, fish, and bean dishes.

**Tarragon**  An aromatic herb with a strong aroma and an assertive flavor reminiscent of anise with undertones of sage. It is widely used in classic French cuisine for chicken, fish, vegetables, and sauces.

**Thyme**  A member of the mint family with a strong, slightly lemony flavor and aroma. It is widely used to flavor vegetables, meat, poultry, fish, soups, and cream sauces. It is basic to French cuisine and integral to bouquet garni.

# Index

251

INDEX

# Order Information

WILD THYME AND OTHER TEMPTATIONS
THE JUNIOR LEAGUE OF TUCSON, INC.
2099 EAST RIVER ROAD
TUCSON, ARIZONA 85718

OFFICE: 520-299-5753
FAX: 520-299-5774

_____
Name

_____
Street Address

_____
City                                State              Zip

_____
Telephone

Please send me _____ copies of *Wild Thyme and Other Temptations* @ $26.95 each   $ _____

Postage and handling @ $4.00 each   $ _____

Total   $ _____

Method of Payment:   [   ] MasterCard      [   ] VISA
[   ] Check payable to The Junior League of Tucson, Inc.

_____
Account Number                          Expiration Date

_____
Cardholder Name

_____
Signature

*Photocopies will be accepted.*